Social Issues
in Literature

Class Conflict in Emily Brontë's *Wuthering Heights*

Other Books in the Social Issues in Literature Series:

Social Issues
in Literature

Class Conflict in Emily Brontë's *Wuthering Heights*

Dedria Bryfonski, Book Editor

GREENHAVEN PRESS
A part of Gale, Cengage Learning

Detroit • New York • San Francisco • New Haven, Conn • Waterville, Maine • London

Christine Nasso, *Publisher*
Elizabeth Des Chenes, *Managing Editor*

© 2011 Greenhaven Press, a part of Gale, Cengage Learning

Gale and Greenhaven Press are registered trademarks used herein under license.

For more information, contact:
Greenhaven Press
27500 Drake Rd.
Farmington Hills, MI 48331-3535
Or you can visit our Internet site at gale.cengage.com

For product information and technology assistance, contact us at

Gale Customer Support, 1-800-877-4253
For permission to use material from this text or product, submit all requests online at
www.cengage.com/permissions

Further permissions questions can be emailed to permissionrequest@cengage.com

Articles in Greenhaven Press anthologies are often edited for length to meet page requirements. In addition, original titles of these works are changed to clearly present the main thesis and to explicitly indicate the author's opinion. Every effort is made to ensure that Greenhaven Press accurately reflects the original intent of the authors. Every effort has been made to trace the owners of copyrighted material.

Cover photograph copyright © Interfoto/Alamy.

LIBRARY OF CONGRESS CATALOGING-IN-PUBLICATION DATA

Class Conflict in Emily Brontë's Wuthering Heights / Dedria Bryfonski, book editor.
        p. cm. -- (Social issues in literature)
    Includes bibliographical references and index.
    ISBN 978-0-7377-5801-6 (hardcover) -- ISBN 978-0-7377-5802-3 (pbk.)
    1. Brontë Emily, 1818-1848. Wuthering Heights. 2. Social conflict in literature.
    PR4172.W73C54 2011
    823'.8--dc22
                                                                    2011009379

Printed in the United States of America
1 2 3 4 5 6 7 15 14 13 12 11

Contents

Chapter 1: Background on Emily Brontë

Relatively little is known about Emily Brontë. She wrote just one novel, the tempestuous masterpiece *Wuthering Heights*, and lived a short, uneventful life. The novel seems to be wholly imaginative, with no autobiographical elements.

Charlotte Brontë claimed that in *Wuthering Heights*, her sheltered and withdrawn sister Emily was describing a setting she had grown up in and knew well, but that she never knew anyone like the passionate and tormented characters described in the novel.

To say that Emily Brontë wrote *Wuthering Heights* from her imagination rather than from her experiences is incorrect. Although she lived a sheltered life, her tormented brother, Branwell, brought chaos and suffering into the family home and provided Emily with a character model.

Chapter 2: *Wuthering Heights* and Class Conflict

Understanding the social changes taking place in England between 1801 and 1847 provides context for an appreciation of *Wuthering Heights*. As industrialization spread, a growing middle class challenged the position of the landed gentry. The Earnshaws and Heathcliff represent this momentum.

Heathcliff and Catherine's rejection of the bourgeois values of Thrushcross Grange symbolizes the conflict in Victorian society between those attempting to preserve class privileges and those attempting to build a classless world.

Wuthering Heights is set during a time when the old social order of rigid class distinctions, importance of heredity, and strict guidelines for the passing down of property within the same class and family were being challenged. Heathcliff leads this challenge successfully.

An unusual aspect of *Wuthering Heights* is the prominent role servants play in the novel. One of the two narrators is the housekeeper, Nelly Dean, who in addition to relating the history of the two families, influences their eventual destinies by her actions.

Chapter 3: Contemporary Perspectives on Class Conflict

Class conflict has replaced racial conflict as the major division in American culture and politics. The gap between rich and poor has widened, resulting in a social chasm that is increasingly difficult to cross.

The victories won by blacks, feminists, Hispanics, and gays have obscured the fact that the major inequality in American society remains. There is a fundamental and lasting divide between the working class and capitalist owners, and no progress is being made to bridge that divide.

Introduction

Emily Brontë's 1847 novel *Wuthering Heights* remains one of the preeminent fictional works in the English language. It powerfully dramatizes the human condition in the doomed relationship between Heathcliff and Cathy. Many critics maintain that the novel is also enriched by the theme of class conflict symbolized in the tensions between the Earnshaws and the Lintons: The orphan Heathcliff awakens a hidden discord, wreaking havoc on two generations. As Arnold Kettle states in *An Introduction to the English Novel*, "*Wuthering Heights* . . . is an expression in the imaginative terms of art of the stresses and tensions and conflicts, personal and spiritual, of nineteenth-century capitalist society."

There is ample evidence in Emily Brontë's life to support her interest in class conflict. Although she and her five siblings lived a sheltered life on the remote Yorkshire moors, they read extensively and were well versed in contemporary politics and events. Their father, Patrick Brontë, was a clergyman who developed a passion for politics after the death of his wife and became an ardent Tory. (At the time, the Tory party upheld traditional conservative values, though Patrick had a strong sympathy for the causes of the poor and also fought for religious freedom.) He maintained a library and had access to the Keighley Mechanics Institute Library, a 300-volume collection he made available to his children. All the Brontë children read political and literary journals and were especially drawn to *Blackwood's Magazine*, a Tory literary and social commentary journal. The oldest daughter, Maria, was given responsibility for entertaining the younger children, which she often did by reading them parliamentary debates from newspapers. Key issues of the times were the Catholic Emancipation, which gave some Catholics the right to vote and enter certain professions, and the Reform Bill of 1832, which extended voting rights to men in newly industrialized cities.

Emily Brontë lived from 1818 to 1848. The events of *Wuthering Heights* take place from 1771 to 1802, a time when political, cultural, and social changes were just beginning to take hold in England. The main cause of these changes was the Industrial Revolution, which began in the late eighteenth century in England when the development of new machinery and production methods changed the economic base of society from rural and agrarian to urban and industrial. This economic shift created a similar social shift. The old class system based on the possession of land was challenged by capitalists, who gained their wealth through industry and manufacturing. Although the Industrial Revolution in England was relatively peaceful and took place gradually over a number of years, England was indirectly affected by more dramatic events occurring in the United States and France. The American Revolution (1775–1783) and the French Revolution (1789–1799) created an atmosphere conducive to democracy and social mobility. These sentiments contributed to the insecurity felt by members of the landed gentry in England.

Brontë's choice of time period was deliberate. In 1847, when she was writing *Wuthering Heights*, the Industrial Revolution was well established in England and had already disrupted the traditional relationship between social classes. By then the ownership of land was no longer the sole means of determining one's place in society; newly acquired wealth could also make a man a gentleman. In 1801, when the novel begins, the traditional gentry were just beginning to be challenged by capitalist upstarts.

According to David Cody, writing for *The Victorian Web*[1],

> Early in the nineteenth century the labels "working classes"
> and "middle classes" were already coming into common us-
> age. The old hereditary aristocracy, reinforced by the new
> gentry who owed their success to commerce, industry, and

the professions, evolved into an "upper class" ... which tenaciously maintained control over the political system, depriving not only the working classes but the middle classes of a voice in the political process. The increasingly powerful (and class conscious) middle classes, however, undertook organized agitation to remedy this situation: The passage of the Reform Act of 1832 and the abolition of the Corn Laws [in force since 1689, these laws protected English landholders by promoting the export and limiting the import of corn] in 1846 were intimations of the extent to which they would ultimately be successful.

In *Wuthering Heights* both the Earnshaws and the Lintons are property owners, but they belong to different classes. The Lintons, living at Thrushcross Grange, are landed gentry and represent convention, tradition, and stability. They are socially superior to the Earnshaws of Wuthering Heights, wealthy farmers who represent uncivilized nature. The interloper Heathcliff has no social standing and no property. It is symbolic of the social change taking place in England that during the course of *Wuthering Heights*, Heathcliff gains possession of both Thrushcross Grange and Wuthering Heights. According to Elisabeth Rose Gruner in *World Literature and Its Times: Profiles of Notable Literary Works and the Historical Events That Influenced Them*:

> Heathcliff represents a threat to the orderly society of Wuthering Heights. His status—as servant or slave—family member or interloper—is continually at issue in the novel. Brontë represents the anxiety of the gentry over the period's new social mobility in the Lintons' distaste for Heathcliff. Ultimately, however, the little society of the novel is able to accommodate upheaval. England in the nineteenth century prided itself on the prudent constitutional and social change that helped it avoid the revolutions that swept the continent, beginning with the French Revolution and continuing

through the 1840s; the society of Wuthering Heights and Thrushcross Grange reenacts this evolutionary change in microcosm.

The essays in *Social Issues in Literature: Class Conflict in Emily Brontë's "Wuthering Heights"* examine class conflict in the novel as well as the manifestations of class conflict in twenty-first century America.

Notes

1. David Cody, "Social Class," *The Victorian Web: Literature, History & Culture in the Age of Victoria*. www.victorianweb.org/history/Class.html.

Chronology

1818

Emily Jane Brontë is born on July 30 in Thornton, Yorkshire, the fifth of six children of Reverend Patrick and Maria Branwell Brontë.

1820

Anne Brontë is born on January 17.

In April the Brontë family moves to Haworth, West Yorkshire, where Patrick Brontë is named curate for life.

1821

Maria Branwell Brontë dies in September. Her sister, Elizabeth Branwell, comes to care for the children.

1824

Emily enrolls at the Clergy Daughters' School in Cowan Bridge in November, joining her older sisters, Maria, Elizabeth, and Charlotte.

1825

The two oldest Brontë sisters, Maria and Elizabeth, die on May 6 and June 15. Charlotte and Emily return home from Cowan Bridge in June.

1826

Returning from a trip to Leeds in June, Patrick brings his children a set of toy wooden soldiers. The children begin creating stories featuring the soldiers in what is now called the Brontë juvenilia.

1831

Charlotte leaves to study at Roe Head School.

Emily and Anne begin writing a fantasy saga called "Gondal."

1834

Emily's earliest known manuscript, which mentions events of the "Gondal" saga, is dated November 24, 1834.

1835

Emily attends Roe Head School from July through October.

1836

The earliest known poem written by Emily is dated July 12.

1837

Emily begins teaching at Law Hill School, a girls' school at Southowram (near Halifax), in September, remaining there for about six months.

1838–42

Emily writes much of her surviving poetry.

1842

With Charlotte, Emily attends Pensionnat Heger in Brussels, where they study music, French, and German. After the death of their aunt Elizabeth Branwell, they return to Haworth.

1845

Emily's brother, Branwell, is dismissed for misconduct from his post as tutor to the Robinson family, beginning his period of deterioration.

In December Emily begins writing *Wuthering Heights*.

1846

Charlotte discovers Emily's hidden poetry. In May it is published with verse by Charlotte and Anne as *Poems by Currer, Ellis, and Acton Bell.*

The three Brontë sisters send manuscripts to potential publishers—Emily sends *Wuthering Heights*; Anne, *Agnes Grey*; and Charlotte, *The Professor.*

1847

Jane Eyre, by Charlotte Brontë, is published in October, and *Wuthering Heights* and *Agnes Grey* are published in December.

1848

Both Branwell and Emily die of consumption—Branwell in September and Emily on December 19.

Anne's *The Tenant of Wildfell Hall* is published.

1849

Anne dies in May.

Charlotte publishes *Shirley*, honoring Emily and Anne.

1850

A new edition of *Wuthering Heights* is published, edited and with a preface by Charlotte.

Social Issues
in Literature

| Background on
| Emily Brontë

The Life of Emily Brontë

Tom Winnifrith

Tom Winnifrith taught for many years in the School of English and Comparative Literature at the University of Warwick, England. A literary critic, he has written numerous books and articles on the Brontës, including The Brontës and Their Background.

According to Winnifrith in the following selection, Emily Brontë led a very sheltered existence. She rarely left the family home in Yorkshire, and, on the few occasions she ventured forth either for education or to teach, she soon returned home. Critics have found it hard to reconcile her limited contact with the larger world with the power, violence, and sophistication of her masterpiece, Wuthering Heights. *Winnifrith argues that unlike the characters of many Victorian novels, those in* Wuthering Heights *are complex individuals who, despite their flaws, retain the reader's sympathy.*

The biographer of Emily Brontë faces considerable problems. Her slender output of one great novel and some impressive but baffling poems does not give one a great deal upon which to build. Unlike her sister Charlotte, whose works do have an autobiographical streak, Emily did not seem to draw upon her own rather humdrum experiences in creating her masterpiece. Attempts to find a real-life Heathcliff in Emily Brontë's Irish forebears or Yorkshire neighbors seem highly speculative. Because Charlotte Brontë won instant fame while she was still alive, far more is known about her life than about Emily's; and it is largely through Charlotte's eyes that Emily is seen: either in incidental references among her correspondence to Ellen Nussey when Emily was alive, or in pious memories when she was dead. Emily Brontë's surviving correspondence is limited to a handful of brief notes, the diary papers she wrote at four-year intervals with her sister Anne, and some exercises she wrote in French in Brussels.

Emily Brontë Spent Most of Her Time at Home

This pathetic paucity of primary evidence has left biographers free to indulge in wild speculation. The temptation to fill the drab life of a genteel English spinster with the wild power of *Wuthering Heights* (1847) is certainly great, but the unadorned facts, insofar as they can be ascertained, may serve to make her imaginative achievement more impressive. Emily Jane Brontë was the fifth child and fourth daughter of the Reverend Patrick Brontë, who moved in April 1820 to the village of Haworth eight miles from Thornton, her birthplace. Emily's mother, who had given birth to her youngest daughter, Anne, on 17 January 1820, died in November 1821, having been ill for several months. Like all the Brontë novels, *Wuthering Heights* has more than its fair share of children who have lost one or both parents.

Faced with the care of six motherless children, Mr. Brontë made efforts to marry again, but soon invited his wife's sister, Elizabeth Branwell, to keep house for him. In July 1824 he sent his two elder daughters, Maria and Elizabeth, to Clergy Daughters' School at Cowan Bridge, Charlotte following in August and Emily in November. In the spring of 1825 there was an epidemic at the school, Maria and Elizabeth died, and Emily and Charlotte were removed from Cowan Bridge. It is difficult to know whether the portrait of Lowood in *Jane Eyre* (1847) is an accurate picture of Cowan Bridge, and although Charlotte clearly was unhappy there, it cannot be known how Emily felt at the age of six. Her subsequent departures from Haworth were brief, and she was not happy away from home.

Emily was indeed at Haworth for the next ten years. In 1826 Mr. Brontë brought home some wooden soldiers, and the precocious children began writing stories about them. With Charlotte and their brother, Branwell, as the main instigators, an imaginary realm in Africa, called Angria, was invented; but at a fairly early stage Emily and Anne broke away and invented their own realm of Gondal, set in the Pacific Ocean. The first of their diary notes, written in November 1834, gives the first mention of Gondal. They continued writing prose and poems about Gondal until the end of their lives. None of the prose has survived, and the poetry, the earliest of which dates to 1836, is difficult to interpret. Various efforts have been made to fit the poems into a coherent saga, but these efforts are probably misguided. Some poems appear not to be about Gondal at all, but rather to reflect Emily's own feelings.

Charlotte had been sent away in 1831 for a year and a half to a school in East Yorkshire run by Miss Wooler. This school was far more pleasant than Cowan Bridge, and Charlotte made some friends there. In July 1835, Charlotte returned to the school as a teacher, taking Emily with her as a pupil; but this economical arrangement was not a success, and Anne replaced Emily. Emily returned to Haworth and found Branwell there. He had made an equally unsuccessful foray in London in an attempt to earn a living as a painter. With Anne and Charlotte away at Miss Wooler's, Emily and Branwell were thrown into each other's company; and although some of Branwell's influence can be detected in Emily's prose and poetry, the theory that he was the real author of *Wuthering Heights* can probably be discounted.

Emily Brontë Was Unsuccessful as a Teacher

In spite of her previous failure, Emily made another attempt to leave home, going as an assistant teacher to Law Hill, a school run by Miss Patchett near Halifax. Charlotte wrote a letter complaining of the harsh conditions under which Emily worked. Her lack of formal education (virtually all her lessons having been taken at home), her shy temperament, and her homesickness would seem to have made Emily far from an ideal teacher, but the slighting nature of Charlotte's remarks made Miss Patchett reluctant to discuss her eccentric but distinguished assistant with subsequent biographers. The date and duration of Emily's stay at Law Hill are still in doubt. The recent discovery that Charlotte's letter, dated by most biographers 2 October 1837, is clearly postmarked 2 October 1838, would seem to fix Emily's stay in the winter of 1838 to 1839. Law Hill is regarded as important for *Wuthering Heights* because a house nearby, High Sunderland Hall, is assumed to be the model for the house known as Wuthering Heights, and it has even been suggested that the germ of the story of Heathcliff was to be found in recollections of a local Halifax character, Jack Sharp. The parallels are not exact, and the other main claimant to being the model of Wuthering Heights, Top Withens, near Haworth, certainly has a situation similar to the lonely house of Emily's novel, although Top Withens itself is too humble to be equated with Wuthering Heights.

Returning to Haworth in 1839 at the age of twenty, Emily continued to write poetry. Her sisters made brief and unsuccessful efforts to become governesses, but Emily remained at home, either because she was the most domesticated of the sisters or because she was the least suited to become a teacher. Her July 1841 birthday note is, however, full of enthusiasm for a project that the Brontës should run their own school at Haworth. In order to achieve this the sisters would need foreign languages, and so in February 1842 Emily and Charlotte set out to Brussels; Anne had obtained a post as a governess for the Robinson family at Thorp Green.

The position of the Brontës at the Pensionnat Heger in Brussels was halfway between those of pupils and teachers. Some reminiscences exist of Emily as a teacher, and not surprisingly her forbidding reserve did not attract her pupils to her. On the other hand, M. [Monsieur] Heger spoke highly of her intellectual gifts as a student, and her surviving exercises show high imaginative power as well as a good command of French. It is not certain how much German Emily learned; critics have perhaps in too facile a fashion seen the influence of German romanticism behind *Wuthering Heights*.

The Brontë Family's Many Disappointments

In November 1842, the Brontës were forced to return home by the death of their aunt. They had previously been shocked by the death of their father's curate, William Weightman, in September, and by the death of their friend Martha Taylor in Brussels. Charlotte returned to Belgium, where she endured much loneliness and the pangs of unrequited love for M. Heger, but Emily remained at home. Their aunt had left the three girls some money, and there are reports of Emily considering the best way of investing it. For most of 1843 Emily was alone with her father, since Branwell had joined Anne at Thorp Green and Charlotte was still in Brussels, from which she returned at the beginning of 1844. In February 1844 Emily copied her poetry down into two notebooks, one of which she entitled *Gondal Poems*. The other notebook would seem to have contained poetry of a subjective nature.

Emily continued to write poetry in 1844 and 1845, and in a diary note in July 1845 refers enthusiastically to Gondal, although Anne is less sanguine. Branwell Brontë returned home in July 1845 (after being dismissed from his post at the Robinsons for some reason too disgraceful for Victorian prudery to make explicit), and for the rest of his life he was a source of constant anxiety to his family. Mr. Brontë's health was also giving cause for concern. The plan to start a school had foundered in 1844 through lack of interest, and both Charlotte, who wrote letters to M. Heger which he refused to answer,

An 1846 oil painting of Emily Brontë, author of the novel Wuthering Heights. © Hulton Archive/Stringer/Getty Images.

and Anne, who had been badly shocked by her experiences at Thorp Green, were in low spirits. It was in these unpromising circumstances that Emily wrote some of her greatest poetry and *Wuthering Heights*. . . .

Wuthering Heights Puzzled Early Reviewers

Unlike Charlotte's *Jane Eyre*, which was an immediate success when it was published by Smith, Elder at about the same time, *Wuthering Heights* was received with bewilderment. Reviewers were baffled and shocked by the story, though some paid tribute to its strange power. Perhaps the poor reception of *Wuthering Heights* prevented Emily from embarking on another novel. A letter from [her publisher, Thomas] Newby, fitting an envelope addressed to Ellis Bell, her pseudonym, and referring to another novel in progress, has been found; but Newby confused all three sisters, and the novel in question may be Anne's *The Tenant of Wildfell Hall*. This novel was published in June 1848, and, though some modern critics have seen it as Anne's answer to Emily's heterodox [unorthodox] views, contemporary reviewers saw *The Tenant of Wildfell Hall* as further evidence of the Brontës' coarseness and immorality.

Meanwhile all was not well with the Brontës' health. Branwell had degenerated badly since 1845, and he died on 24 September 1848. His physical and spiritual welfare must have caused anxiety for all three sisters, and there are stories of Emily, the tallest of the three, bearing the brunt of looking after him and carrying him about. Anne's health had also been worrying Charlotte, but on 9 October Emily was reported as having a cough and a cold. She struggled through her normal household tasks until almost the day of her death, refusing, according to the popular legend, all medical aid. Her death came very suddenly on 19 December 1848, and she was buried three days later at Haworth.

It is difficult to get any clear impression of Emily's personality or even her personal appearance from the scanty evidence available. Contemporary portraits, not very well authenticated, show Emily in different guises; a certain amount of romanticizing must be allowed for in these pictures. Contemporary accounts suggest that she made no effort to present herself in an attractive fashion. Charlotte Brontë remarked rather oddly that her sister resembled [English philosopher and critic] G.H. Lewes, the husband in all but name of [English author] George Eliot, although portraits of Emily and

Lewes do not seem to bring out the resemblance. Charlotte's memories of her sister, and in particular her remark that the portrait of Shirley in her 1849 novel of the same name was based upon Emily, are likely to have been influenced by a pious wish to speak well of the dead. Emily's originality is borne out by her novel, but tributes to her strength of character ignore the fact that she seemed almost unable to survive outside Haworth. A certain amount of sentimentality must also be allowed for in the picture of Emily working closely in harmony with her two sisters: this picture would seem to be contradicted by the anger of Emily at the discovery of her poems, and by the fact that Anne Brontë, both in her poetry and her second novel, appears to be trying to refute Emily's views. Charlotte's desire to speak highly of her dead sister is of course both understandable and creditable; less creditable has been the refusal of many modern biographers to abandon the hushed superlatives and to admit that Emily, like many great artists, would appear to have had a rather difficult personality. . . .

Emily Brontë's Fiction Is at Odds with Her Placid Life

Emily Brontë remains enigmatic because so little is known about her, and what is known is contradictory. Her life seems one of dreary conformity; her book seems designed to outrage and shock. Even the modern reader, whose susceptibility to shock must be less than that of his Victorian counterpart, is still outraged not so much by the violence of word, deed, and atmosphere as by the sudden surprise to his sensibilities when he finds characters appealing to him in spite of what they do. Perhaps the only certain message of *Wuthering Heights* is that nothing is certain. Brontë's defiance of rigid categories and her refusal to divide people into saints and sinners, gentry and servants, good and bad is very un-Victorian, but does not seem out of keeping with what is known of her temperament.

Heathcliff's cruelty and Cathy's selfishness do not prevent them from being attractive. The Lintons are spoiled and weak, but Isabella's and her son's sufferings and Edgar's devotion to his wife win them sympathy. Hindley is profligate and cruel, neglecting even Hareton in a shocking fashion; but Nelly Dean, who is Hindley's foster sister and has an old retainer's [servant's] loyalty, finds a mournful pathos about his fall and inspires the reader to do the same. Joseph, the servant at Wuthering Heights, is hypocritical, pharisaical [strict in his religion], a believer in hell fire and predestination. Brontë would appear to have believed in truth, tolerance, and universal salvation. Yet it is one of the oddest features of the novel that one feels that Joseph, who is always present at Wuthering Heights, is somehow akin to Brontë in his savage contempt for almost everything and his belief that gloom is good for the soul.

Heathcliff himself, at first sight so straight an unredeemed villain or Byronic [idealized but flawed] hero [in the style of poet Lord Byron's characters], acts at times in a surprising fashion. One can never quite make out the significance of the episodes in which he catches Hareton when Hindley drunkenly drops him over the banisters, or in which—spitting and cursing—he prevents Hindley from bleeding to death, although he has threatened to kill Hindley and Hindley has just tried to kill him. It is odd, too, to find Heathcliff offering to make a cup of tea for Nelly Dean and Catherine at a time when he is acting villainously toward both of them. These touches of humanity prevent Heathcliff and *Wuthering Heights* from lapsing into unrealistic melodrama; one is reminded of the sudden unexpected words in Brontë's poetry, and homely glimpses of the authoress of *Wuthering Heights* baking the bread.

Heathcliff stands unredeemed, says Charlotte Brontë in her introduction to the second edition, but qualifies her remark by saying that his affection for Hareton partially redeems him. She then gives a surprising hint about the origins of Heathcliff's name. Most readers will think of a heath as an arid waste as in [William Shakespeare's play] *King Lear*, and there are plenty of barren wastes on the moors near Wuthering Heights and in Heathcliff's heart. But there is also a small flower named a heath, and it is to this that Charlotte links the mighty and rugged cliff that stands for *Wuthering Heights*. Emily Brontë would appear to be a wilting flower who created a mighty rock.

Emily Brontë Wrote About a Countryside She Knew and People She Imagined

Charlotte Brontë

An older sister of Emily Brontë, Charlotte Brontë was an English writer and the author of the novel Jane Eyre.

In the following viewpoint, Charlotte Brontë provides her perspective on how her sheltered sister was able to create the power and passion of Wuthering Heights. *Emily Brontë was at home in the Yorkshire moors and used that rough countryside to set the mood and character of her novel, states Charlotte. However, her sister was uncomfortable in society and had no experience with the tortured souls who appear in* Wuthering Heights. *Charlotte claims that such characters as Heathcliff and Catherine sprang fully from her imagination and not from her personal experience.*

I have just read over *Wuthering Heights*, and, for the first time, have obtained a clear glimpse of what are termed (and, perhaps, really are) its faults; have gained a definite notion of how it appears to other people—to strangers who knew nothing of the author; who are unacquainted with the locality where the scenes of the story are laid; to whom the inhabitants, the customs, the natural characteristics of the outlying hills and hamlets in the West Riding of Yorkshire are things alien and unfamiliar.

Charlotte Brontë, "A Spirit More Sombre Than Sunny, More Powerful Than Sportive," *Emily Brontë: Wuthering Heights: A Casebook*, Houndmills, Basingstoke, Hampshire, and London: Macmillan, 1992, pp.60–64. Copyright © 1992. All rights reserved. Reproduced by permission.

The Wildness of Yorkshire
Is Accurately Described

To all such *Wuthering Heights* must appear a rude and strange production. The wild moors of the north of England can for them have no interest; the language, the manners, the very dwellings and household customs of the scattered inhabitants of those districts, must be to such readers in a great measure unintelligible, and—where intelligible—repulsive. Men and women who, perhaps naturally very calm, and with feelings moderate in degree, and little marked in kind, have been trained from their cradle to observe the utmost evenness of manner and guardedness of language, will hardly know what to make of the rough, strong utterance, the harshly manifested passions, the unbridled aversions, and headlong partialities of unlettered moorland hinds [English farm workers] and rugged moorland squires, who have grown up untaught and un-checked, except by mentors as harsh as themselves. A large class of readers, likewise, will suffer greatly from the introduc-tion into the pages of this work of words printed with all their letters, which it has become the custom to represent by the initial and final letter only—a blank line filling the inter-val. I may as well say at once that, for this circumstance, it is out of my power to apologise; deeming it, myself, a rational plan to write words at full length. The practice of hinting by single letters those expletives with which profane and violent persons are wont to garnish their discourse, strikes me as a proceeding which, however well meant, is weak and futile, I cannot tell what good it does—what feeling it spares—what horror it conceals.

With regard to the rusticity of *Wuthering Heights*, I admit the charge, for I feel the quality. It is rustic all through. It is moorish, and wild, and knotty as a root of heath. Nor was it natural that it should be otherwise; the author being herself a native and nursling of the moors. Doubtless, had her lot been cast in a town, her writings, if she had written at all, would have possessed another character. Even had chance or taste led her to choose a similar subject, she would have treated it otherwise. Had Ellis Bell [Emily's pseudonym] been a lady or a gentleman accustomed to what is called 'the world', her view of a remote and unreclaimed region, as well as of the dwellers therein, would have differed greatly from that actually taken by the homebred country girl. Doubtless it would have been wider—more comprehensive: whether it would have been more original or more truthful is not so certain. As far as the scenery and locality are concerned, it could scarcely have been so sympathetic: Ellis Bell did not describe as one whose eye and taste alone found pleasure in the prospect; her native hills were far more to her than a spectacle; they were what she lived in, and by, as much as the wild birds, their tenants, or as the heather, their produce. Her descriptions, then, of natural scenery, are what they should be, and all they should be.

Emily Brontë Was Shy and Reclusive

Where delineation of human character is concerned, the case is different. I am bound to avow that she had scarcely more practical knowledge of the peasantry amongst whom she lived, than a nun has of the country people who sometimes pass her convent gates. My sister's disposition was not naturally gregarious; circumstances favoured and fostered her tendency to seclusion; except to go to church or take a walk on the hills, she rarely crossed the threshold of home. Though her feeling for the people round was benevolent, intercourse with them she never sought; nor, with very few exceptions, ever experienced. And yet she knew them: knew their ways, their language, their family histories; she could hear of them with interest, and talk of them with details, minute, graphic, and accurate; but *with* them, she rarely exchanged a word. Hence it ensued that what her mind had gathered of the real concerning them, was too exclusively confined to those tragic and terrible traits of which, in listening to the secret annals of every rude vicinage [neighborhood], the memory is sometimes compelled to receive the impress. Her imagination, which was a spirit more sombre than sunny, more powerful than sportive, found in such traits material whence it wrought creations like Heathcliff, like Earnshaw, like Catherine. Having formed these beings she did not know what she had done. If the auditor of her work, when read in manuscript, shuddered under the grinding influence of natures so relentless and implacable, of spirits so lost and fallen; if it was complained that the mere hearing of certain vivid and fearful scenes banished sleep by night, and disturbed mental peace by day, Ellis Bell would wonder what was meant, and suspect the complainant of affectation. Had she but lived, her mind would of itself have grown like a strong tree, loftier, straighter, wider-spreading, and its matured fruits would have attained a mellower ripeness and sunnier bloom; but on that mind time and experience alone could work: to the influence of other intellects, it was not amenable [open].

Nelly Dean Is Admirable, Heathcliff Is Demonic

Having avowed that over much of *Wuthering Heights* there broods 'a horror of great darkness'; that, in its storm-heated and electrical atmosphere, we seem at times to breathe lightning, let me point to those spots where clouded daylight and the eclipsed sun still attest their existence. For the specimen of true benevolence and homely fidelity, look at the character of Nelly Dean; for an example of constancy and tenderness, remark that of Edgar Linton. (Some people will think these qualities do not shine so well incarnate in a man as they would do in a woman, but Ellis Bell could never be brought to comprehend this notion: nothing moved her more than any insinuation that the faithfulness and clemency, the long-suffering and loving kindness which are esteemed virtues in the daughters of Eve, become foibles in the sons of Adam. She

Portrait of Emily Brontë, painted by her sister Charlotte Brontë circa 1835. © Rischgitz/ Stringer/Getty Images.

held that mercy and forgiveness are the divinest attributes of the Great Being who made both man and woman, and that what clothes the Godhead in glory, can disgrace no form of feeble humanity.) There is a dry saturnine [surly] humour in the delineation of old Joseph, and some glimpses of grace and gaiety animate the younger Catherine. Nor is even the first heroine of the name destitute of a certain strange beauty in her fierceness, or of honesty in the midst of perverted passion and passionate perversity.

Heathcliff, indeed, stands unredeemed; never once swerving in his arrow-straight course to perdition, from the time when 'the little black-haired swarthy thing, as dark as if it came from the Devil', was first unrolled out of the bundle and set on its feet in the farmhouse kitchen, to the hour when Nelly Dean found the grim, stalwart corpse laid on its back in the panel-enclosed bed, with wide-gazing eyes that seemed 'to sneer at her attempt to close them, and parted lips and sharp white teeth that sneered too'.

Heathcliff betrays one solitary human feeling, and that is *not* his love for Catherine; which is a sentiment fierce and inhuman; a passion such as might boil and glow in the bad essence of some evil genres; a fire that might form the tormented centre—the ever-suffering soul of a magnate [powerful figure] of the internal world: and by its quenchless and ceaseless ravage effect the execution of the decree which dooms him to carry Hell with him wherever he wanders. No; the single link that connects Heathcliff with humanity is his rudely-confessed regard for Hareton Earnshaw—the young man who he has ruined; and then his half-implied esteem for Nelly Dean. These solitary traits omitted, we should say he was child neither of Lascar [Indian army servant] nor gipsy, but a man's shape animated by demon life—a Ghoul—an Afreet [evil genie].

The Artist's Limited Power

Whether it is right or advisable to create beings like Heathcliff, I do not know: I scarcely think it is. But this I know: the writer who possesses the creative gift owns something of which he is not always master—something that, at times, strangely wills and works for itself. He may lay down rules and devise principles, and to rules and principles it will perhaps for years lie in subjection; and then, haply without any warning of revolt, there comes a time when it will no longer consent to 'harrow [plow] the valleys, or be bound with a band in the furrow'—when it 'laughs at the multitude of the city, and regards not the crying of the driver'—when, refusing absolutely to make ropes out of sea-sand any longer, it sets to work in statue-hewing, and you have a Pluto or a Jove, a Tisiphone or a Psyche, a Mermaid or a Madonna, as Fate or Inspiration direct. Be the work grim or glorious, dread or divine, you have little choice left but quiescent [obedient] adoption. As for you—the nominal [supposed] artist—your share in it has been to work passively under dictates you neither delivered nor could question—that would not be uttered at your prayer, nor suppressed nor changed at your caprice. If the result be attractive, the World will praise you, who little deserve praise; if it be repulsive, the same World will blame you, who almost as little deserve blame.

Wuthering Heights was hewn in a wild workshop, with simple tools, out of homely materials. The statuary found a granite block on a solitary moor; gazing thereon, he saw how from the crag might be elicited a head, savage, swart, sinister; a form moulded with at least one element of grandeur— power. He wrought with a rude chisel, and from no model but the vision of his meditations. With time and labour, the crag took human shape; and there it stands colossal, dark, and frowning, half statue, half rock: in the former sense, terrible and goblin-like; in the latter, almost beautiful, for its colouring is of mellow grey, and moorland moss clothes it; and heath, with its blooming bells and balmy fragrance, grows faithfully close to the giant's foot.

Branwell Brontë Was the Inspiration for Heathcliff

A. Mary F. Robinson

A. Mary F. Robinson was a nineteenth-century English poet, novelist, biographer, translator, and literary critic.

Although she led a cloistered existence, Emily Brontë used experiences from her life to create Wuthering Heights, *explains Robinson in this selection. The daughter of a clergyman, she nevertheless rejected the rigid doctrine of Calvinism (the religious inclination of her era), which stresses the absolute authority of God and the depravity of humans. This unorthodoxy is at the heart of her novel. Robinson argues that Emily's brother Branwell had no part in writing* Wuthering Heights, *despite the arguments of some critics. Instead, Emily used her brother's tortured existence as a model for Heathcliff's anguished life.*

A gray old Parsonage standing among graves, remote from the world on its wind-beaten hilltop, all round the neighboring summits wild with moors; a lonely place among half-dead ash-trees and stunted thorns, the world cut off on one side by the still ranks of the serried [crowded] dead, and distanced on the other by mile-long stretches of heath: such, we know, was Emily Brontë's home.

An Inauspicious Background for a Novelist

An old, blind, disillusioned father, once prone to an extraordinary violence of temper, but now grown quiet with age, showing his disappointment with life by a melancholy cynicism that was quite sincere; two sisters, both beloved, one, fired with genius and quick to sentiment, hiding her enthusiasm

A. Mary F. Robinson, "*Wuthering Heights*: Its Origin," *Emily Brontë*, Boston: Roberts Brothers, 1883, pp. 206–207, 209–218.

under the cold demeanor of the ex-governess, unsuccessful, and unrecognized; the other gentler, dearer, fairer, slowly dying, inch by inch, of the blighting neighborhood of vice; one brother, scarce less dear, of set purpose drinking himself to death out of furious thwarted passion for a mistress that he might not marry: these were the members of Emily Brontë's household.

Herself we know: inexperienced, courageous, passionate, and full of pity. Was it wonderful that she summed up life in one bitter line?—

"Conquered good and conquering ill."

Her own circumstances proved the axiom true, and of other lives she had but little knowledge. Whom should she ask? The gentle Ellen [Nussey; a close friend of Charlotte Brontë and correspondent with Emily] who seemed of another world, and yet had plentiful troubles of her own? The curates she despised for their narrow priggishness? The people in the village of whom she knew nothing save when sickness, wrong, or death summoned her to their homes to give help and protection? Her life had given only one view of the world, and she could not realize that there were others which she had not seen.

"I am bound to avow," says Charlotte, "that she had scarcely more practical knowledge of the peasantry among whom she lived than a nun has of the country people that pass her convent gates. My sister's disposition was not naturally gregarious; circumstances favored and fostered her tendency to seclusion; except to go to church, or to take a walk on the hills, she rarely crossed the threshold of home. . . ."

The Significance of Brontë's Environment

Yet no human being is wholly free, none wholly independent, of surroundings. And Emily Brontë least of all could claim such immunity. We can with difficulty just imagine her a prosperous heiress, loving and loved, high-spirited and even hoydenish [boisterous]; but with her cavalier fantasy informed by a gracious splendor all her own, we can just imagine Emily Brontë as Shirley Keeldar [the title character of Charlotte Brontë's novel *Shirley*, who Charlotte claimed was based on Emily] but scarcely Shirley Keeldar writing *Wuthering Heights*. Emily Brontë away from her moors, her loneliness, her poverty, her discipline, her companionship with genius, violence, and degradation, would have taken another color, as hydrangeas grow now red, now blue, according to the nature of the soil. It was not her lack of knowledge of the world that made the novel she wrote become *Wuthering Heights*, not her inexperience, but rather her experience, limited and perverse, indeed, and specialized by a most singular temperament, yet close and very real. Her imagination was as much inspired by the circumstances of her life, as was Anne's when she wrote *The Tenant of Wildfell Hall*, or Charlotte's in her masterpiece *Villette*; but, as in each case the imagination was of a different quality, experience, acting upon it, produced a distinct and dissimilar result; a result obtained no less by the contrariety than by the harmony of circumstance. For our surroundings affect us in two ways; subtly and permanently, tingeing us through and through as wine tinges water, or, by some violent neighborhood of antipathetic force, sending us off at a tangent as far as possible from the antagonistic presence that so detestably environs us. The fact that Charlotte Brontë knew chiefly clergymen is largely responsible for *Shirley*, that satirical eulogy of [tribute to] the Church and apotheosis [glorification] of Sunday-school teachers. But Emily, living in this same clerical evangelistic atmosphere, is revolted, forced to the other extreme; and, while sheltering her true opinions from herself under the all-embracing term "Broad Church" [a more liberal interpretation of the Anglicanism of the Church of England], we find in her writings no belief so strong as the belief in the present use and glory of life; no love so great as her love for earth—earth the mother and grave; no assertion of immortality, but a deep certainty of rest. There is no note so often struck in all her work, and struck with such variety of emphasis, as this: that good for goodness' sake is desirable, evil for evil's sake detestable, and that for the just and the un-just alike there is rest in the grave.

The Rejection of Calvinism

This quiet clergyman's daughter, always hearing evil of Dis-senters [those who disagreed with the established Church of England], has therefore from pure courage and revolted jus-tice become a dissenter herself. A dissenter in more ways than one. Never was a nature more sensitive to the stupidities and narrowness of conventional opinion, a nature more likely to be found in the ranks of the opposition; and with such a na-ture indignation is the force that most often looses the gate of speech. The impulse to reveal wrongs and sufferings as they really are is overwhelmingly strong; although the revelation it-self be imperfect. What, then, would this inexperienced York-shire parson's daughter reveal? The unlikeness of life to the authorized pictures of life; the force of evil, only conquerable by the slow-revolving process of nature which admits not the eternal duration of the perverse; the grim and fearful lessons of heredity; the sufficiency of the finite to the finite, of life to life, with no other reward than the conduct of life fulfils to him that lives; the all-penetrating kinship of living things, heather-sprig, singing lark, confident child, relentless tyrant; and, not least, not least to her already in its shadow, the sure and universal peace of death.

A strange evangel [gospel] from such a preacher; but a faith evermore emphasized and deeper rooted in Emily's mind by her incapacity to acquiesce in the stiff, pragmatic teaching, the narrow prejudice, of the Calvinists of Haworth. Yet this very Calvinism influenced her ideas, this doctrine she so pas-sionately rejected, calling herself a disciple of the tolerant and thoughtful [English theologian] Frederick Maurice, and writing, in defiance of its flames and shriekings, the most soothing consolations to mortality that I remember in our tongue.

Evil Will Not Follow Heathcliff to the Grave

Nevertheless, so dual-natured is the force of environment, this antagonistic faith, repelling her to the extreme rebound of belief, did not send her out from it before she had assimilated some of its sternest tenets. From this doctrine of reward and punishment she learned that for every unchecked evil tendency there is a fearful expiation [punishment]; though she placed it not indeed in the flames of hell, but in the perverted instincts of our own children. Terrible theories of doomed incurable sin and predestined loss warned her that an evil stock will only beget contamination: the children of the mad must be liable to madness; the children of the depraved, bent towards depravity; the seed of the poison-plant springs up to blast and ruin, only to be overcome by uprooting and sterilization, or by the judicious grafting, the patient training of many years.

Thus prejudiced and evangelical Haworth had prepared the woman who rejected its Hebraic [characteristic of Jewish theology integrated into Christianity] dogma, to find out for herself the underlying truths. She accepted them in their full significance. It has been laid as a blame to her that she nowhere shows any proper abhorrence of the fiendish and vindictive Heathcliff. She who reveals him remembers the dubious parentage of that forsaken seaport baby, "Lascar or Gipsy" [a phrase from Charlotte Brontë's introduction to the 1850 edition of *Wuthering Heights;* a Lascar was a sailor native to India]; she remembers the Ishmaelitish [outcast] childhood, too much loved and hated, of the little interloper whose hand was against every man's hand. Remembering this, she submits as patiently to his swarthy soul and savage instincts as to his swarthy skin and "gibberish that nobody could understand." From thistles [which are prickly] you gather no grapes.

No use, she seems to be saying, in waiting for the children of evil parents to grow, of their own will and unassisted, straight and noble. The very quality of their will is as inherited as their eyes and hair. Heathcliff is no fiend or goblin; the untrained doomed child of some half-savage sailor's holiday, violent and treacherous. And how far shall we hold the sinner responsible for a nature which is itself the punishment of some forefather's crime? Even for such there must be rest. No possibility in the just and reverent mind of Emily Brontë that the God whom she believed to be the very fount and soul of life could condemn to everlasting fire the victims of morbid tendencies not chosen by themselves. No purgatory, and no everlasting flame, is needed to purify the sins of Heathcliff; his grave on the hillside will grow as green as any other spot of grass, moor-sheep will find the grass as sweet, heath and hare-bells will grow of the same color on it as over a baby's grave. For life and sin and punishment end with death to the dying man; he slips his burden then on to other shoulders, and no visions mar his rest.

"I wondered how any one could ever imagine unquiet slumbers for the sleepers in that quiet earth." So ends the last page of *Wuthering Heights*.

The Role of Branwell Brontë in *Wuthering Heights*

So much for theories of life and evil that the clash of circumstance and character struck out from Emily Brontë. It happened, as we know, that she had occasion to test these theories; and but for that she could never have written *Wuthering Heights*. Not that the story, the conception, would have failed. After all there is nothing more appalling in the violent history of that upland farm than many a mid-land manor set thick in elms, many a wild country-house of Wales or Cornwall, could unfold. Stories more socially painful than the mere brute violence of the Earnshaws; of madness and treachery, stories of girls entrapped unwillingly into a lunatic marriage that the estate might have an heir; legends of fearful violence, of outcast children, dishonored wives, horrible and persistent evil. Who, in the secret places of his memory, stores not up such haunting gossip? And Emily, familiar with all the wild stories of Haworth for a century back, and nursed on grisly Irish horrors, tales of [an Irish uprising in] 1798, tales of oppression and misery, Emily, with all this eerie lore at her finger-ends, would have the less difficulty in combining and working the separate motives into a consistent whole, that she did not know the real people whose histories she knew by heart. No memory of individual manner, dominance or preference for an individual type, caught and disarranged her theories, her conception being the completer from her ignorance. This much her strong reason and her creative power enabled her to effect. But this is not all.

This is the plot; but to make a character speak, act, rave, love, live, die, through a whole lifetime of events, even as the readers feel convinced he must have acted, must have lived and died, this demands at least so much experience of a somewhat similar nature as may serve for a base to one's imagination, a reserve of certainty and reassurance on which to draw in times of perplexity and doubt. Branwell, who sat to Anne sorrily enough for the portrait of Henry Huntingdon [an English clergyman and historian of the eleventh century] served his sister Emily, not indeed as a model, a thing to copy, but as a chart of proportions by which to measure, and to which to refer, for correct investiture [formation], the inspired idea. [English journalist, novelist, and biographer] Mr. Wemyss Reid (whose great knowledge of the Brontë history and still greater kindness in admitting me to his advantages as much as might be, I cannot sufficiently acknowledge)—this capable critic perceives a *bonâ fide* resemblance between the character of Heathcliff and the character of Branwell Brontë as he appeared to his sister Emily. So much, bearing in mind the verse concerning the leveret [young hare], I own I cannot see. Branwell seems to me more nearly akin to Heathcliff's miserable son than to Heathcliff. But that, in depicting Heathcliff's outrageous thwarted love for Catharine, Emily did draw upon her experience of her brother's suffering, this extract from an unpublished lecture of Mr. Reid's will sufficiently reveal:

"It was in the enforced companionship of this lost and degraded man that Emily received, I am sure, many of the impressions which were subsequently conveyed to the pages of her book. Has it not been said over and over again by critics of every kind that *Wuthering Heights* reads like the dream of an opium-eater? And here we find that during the whole time of the writing of the book an habitual and avowed opium-eater was at Emily's elbow I said that perhaps the most striking part of *Wuthering Heights* was that which deals with the relations of Heathcliff and Catharine after she had become the wife of another. Whole pages of the story are filled with the ravings and ragings of the villain against the man whose life stands between him and the woman he loves. Similar ravings are to be found in all the letters of Branwell Brontë written at this period of his career; and we may be sure that similar ravings were always on his lips as, moody and more than half mad, he wandered about the rooms of the parsonage at Haworth. Nay, I have found some striking verbal coincidences between Branwell's own language and passages in *Wuthering Heights*. In one of his own letters there are these words in reference to the object of his passion: My own life without her will be hell. What can the so-called love of her wretched sickly husband be to her compared with mine?' Now, turn to *Wuthering Heights* and you will read these words: Two words would comprehend my future—death and hell; existence after losing her would be hell. Yet I was a fool to fancy for a moment that she valued Edgar Linton's attachment more than mine. If he loved with all the powers of his puny being, he couldn't love in eighty years as much as I could in a day.'"

So much share in *Wuthering Heights* Branwell certainly had. He was a page of the book in which his sister studied; he served, as to an artist's temperament all things unconsciously serve, for the rough block of granite out of which the work is hewn, and, even while with difficulty enduring his vices, Emily undoubtedly learned from them those darker secrets of humanity necessary to her tragic incantation. They served her, those dreaded, passionate outbreaks of her brother's, even as the moors she loved, the fancy she courted, served her. Strange divining wand of genius, that conjures gold out of the miriest [muddiest] earth of common life; strange and terrible faculty laying up its stores and half-mechanically drawing its own profit out of our slightest or most miserable experiences, noting the gesture with which the mother hears of her son's ruin, catching the faint varying shadow that the white wind-shaken window-blind sends over the dead face by which we watch, drawing its life from a thousand deaths, humiliations, losses, with a hand in our sharpest joys and bitterest sorrows; this faculty was Emily Brontë's, and drew its profit from her brother's shame.

Social Issues
in Literature

CHAPTER 2

Wuthering Heights and Class Conflict

Wuthering Heights Reflects the Social Changes of Its Time

Beth Newman

Beth Newman is an associate professor of English at Southern Methodist University. She is the author of Subjects on Display: Psychoanalysis, Social Expectation, and Victorian Femininity *and the editor of a 1996 edition of* Jane Eyre.

In the following viewpoint, Newman stresses that to fully appreciate the subtleties of Wuthering Heights, *students must understand the wave of industrialism that swept over Victorian England and the changes it made to the social structure. With this understanding, she asserts, it is possible for students to grasp that the interpersonal drama between members of the Earnshaw and Linton families represents the larger social conflict in English society during this era.*

Emily Brontë's operatic representations of passion have encouraged critics to describe her novel [*Wuthering Heights*] as mythological and cosmic or timeless and metaphysical. (Significantly, Terry Eagleton's project in *Myths of Power* is not to correct this perception but to explain why Brontë turned to myth in exploring the tensions she probed.) The story of two houses nearly destroyed by unconsummated desire and virulent hatred has widespread appeal in our time, and its archetypal [having symbolism that is universally familiar] plots of an outsider wreaking havoc on a community and of calculated, protracted revenge lend themselves to adaptations in many different cultural milieus. Filmmakers have retold the story of the first generation of Earnshaws and Lintons in settings as removed from the remote Yorkshire moors as medieval Japan, a Mexican chaparral, and upper-caste India. Students respond to the mythic quality of *Wuthering Heights* and they should be encouraged to recognize and enjoy it. But we can and should help them understand the novel as a fictive engagement with a specific social world. We can demonstrate that Brontë's novel grapples with the conflicts and contradictions of mid-Victorian England—that rather than stand aloof from nineteenth-century discursive [ideological] currents or tendencies, it participates in them and contributed to them.

Industrialism in England Challenged the Social Hierarchy

I like to open classroom discussion by asking about the changes that took place in England between 1801, the date of the framing story provided by Lockwood's diary, and 1847, the year of the novel's publication. This approach invites the class to ponder the many possible contexts while fleshing out some of the defining features of life in the early nineteenth century. My students can usually point to the spread of industrialization or, if they have taken our British literature survey, to the Reform Act of 1832 [an act of British Parliament that expanded the right to vote and increased the representation of larger, more industrialized cities]. I develop such references into a broad socioeconomic context by bringing up the political challenge that new urban and industrial interests posed to the traditional authority of landed proprietors like the Lintons, whose power the Reform Act worked to strengthen. It is also useful to make clear that Haworth [the town in which the Brontës lived] was by no means immune to the social and material pressures by industrialism: [historian] Juliet Barker reports in *The Brontës* (1994) that by the time Patrick Brontë arrived at Haworth with his family in 1820, there were already thirteen woolen mills and more than once during Emily's lifetime, Haworth and neighboring Keighley experienced severe unemployment, industrial poverty, and Chartist [social reform movement] agitation.

My goals in providing such information for my students are to foreground the contending social forces produced by the spread of industrialism and to set up the novel's representation of domestic life as a microcosm of the changing relations of class and power in English society as a whole. A little reflection on the technological advances that made industrialization possible may lead students to think about the age of steam and the building of the railroads—and therefore about the accelerated pace of travel and the consequent sense of England as a much smaller place by mid-century than at its beginning, when Lockwood makes his journey to the north of England, or for that matter in the 1770s, when Mr. Earnshaw traverses the sixty miles to Liverpool on foot. These were not academic matters to Emily Brontë. Her brother, Branwell, held a small administrative post on the new Leeds and Manchester Railway in the early 1840s, and the boom years of railway construction, 1844–49, coincide with the writing and publication of the novel. The making of a fairly homogeneous national culture by mid-century and the consequent weakening of regional differences serve as my second context.

I make it clear that other contexts are possible and that they, can illuminate *Wuthering Heights* in different ways. As I solicit the class's input about changes between 1801 and 1847, students frequently mention Liverpool, the city to which Mr. Earnshaw travels. They may be able to link this thriving port with the global commerce of a growing empire and perhaps even with the transatlantic slave trade. According to [critic] Maja-Lisa Von Sneidern, Liverpool's role in the slave trade, already significant at the time of Mr. Earnshaw's journey there, had surpassed that of other English ports by the early nineteenth century. The trade and then slavery itself were abolished in the British Empire in 1807 and 1833, respectively.

Framing *Wuthering Heights* in this context, Von Sneidern offers a compelling reading that posits African origins for Heathcliff and interprets the novel's depiction of romantic love as an eroticized master-slave dialectic, which she links to early nineteenth-century discourse about slavery. In introductory classes, I am more apt to mention this context than to develop it in detail, in part because I think it important to keep the question of Heathcliff's otherness as open as the text does itself. One way of doing so, however, is to entertain the possibility that Heathcliff has African origins. . . .

Wuthering Heights Depicts a Middle-Class Family

The novel's evocations of everyday life at Wuthering Heights reveal the unfolding of social change in both its temporal and geopolitical aspects, but readers not schooled in thinking about the sociohistorical contexts of fiction are likely to overlook the relevant details. [Critics] Sandra M. Gilbert and Susan Gubar have observed that when Hindley returns from college after Mr. Earnshaw's death, he has acquired not only a wife but also new ways of dressing and speaking; in addition, he banishes the servants to the "back-kitchen" and contemplates converting, a spare room into a wallpapered, carpeted parlor. It's useful to draw attention to these details and to ask students to consider their social significance. "College" takes Hindley south, whether to Oxford or Cambridge; there he presumably learns to speak the received Midlands standard [a dialect of a higher class than that spoken in Yorkshire] and to dress in a more genteel fashion. By segregating the servants, Hindley makes their labor less visible and creates a sharper distinction in everyday life between kin and other members of the household. This change makes it easy for him to reclassify Heathcliff as a servant and to impose the illusion of racial as well as class homogeneity [uniformity] onto the relatively heterogeneous [varied] social reality that undergirds both his household and the developing national consciousness.

More concretely, Hindley has reorganized life in his farmhouse so that it more closely resembles the domestic space of the evolving middle-class family, a space that by Emily Brontë's day had become the idealized, sentimentalized Victorian home. I remind students that contrary to the *Flintstones'* portrayal of a Stone Age bourgeois family in a cave, normative middle-class family structure is not timeless. It emerged between the earliest events in *Wuthering Heights* and Emily Brontë's childhood, that is, in the later eighteenth and early nineteenth centuries; it evolved as the manufacture of commodities moved out of and away from the home and as income-generating work became, among the middling ranks, almost the exclusive province of men. By 1847 this arrangement stood as the dominant family form, but in rural England of the 1770s it was only beginning to emerge.

Certainly for American students it helps to sort out the social distinction between the Earnshaws and the Lintons, especially because the houses are presented in such stark opposition that students may underestimate the Earnshaws' position. Nelly observes that Wuthering Heights is the "next best [house] in the neighborhood" after Thrushcross Grange; Eagleton identifies the Earnshaws with the yeomanry, a class of independent, often prosperous farmers who owned their land and were their own masters. Their ways of life and values differed from those of gentry like the Lintons, as suggested by the contrasting interiors of the houses and the presence on the Linton estate of a park—that is, land given over to leisure rather than to agriculture. Moreover, as Nelly tells Lockwood, Edgar "had a sweet, low manner of speaking, and pronounced his words as you do." With the significance of these differences clarified, students can recognize the importance of Hindley's self-fashioning: he seeks to reduce the superficial signs of social distinction between himself and the gentry.

Cathy's Choice Reveals Class Prejudices

This is a good time to raise the question of Cathy's choice of Edgar over Heathcliff and to look closely at Nelly's "catechism" [moral questioning] of her in chapter 9. Many of my students are critical of Cathy's choice, pointing out the glibness of her answers to Nelly's question about why she loves Edgar, her acknowledgment that she is wrong to marry him, and what her language reveals about how fully she has bought into the project of upward mobility: "It would degrade me to marry Heathcliff, now"—now that Hindley has brought him so low and now that she has been transformed from a "wild, hatless little savage" to a "dignified person" with higher prospects. One can complicate this critical view (or encourage others to do so) by emphasizing Cathy's reasonable fear of being reduced to poverty and by invoking the incestuous status of the fierce attachment between Heathcliff and Cathy. Nelly's objection that Cathy might meet another handsome, rich man is worth considering, too. In theory, she might, but her situation makes it unlikely: Cathy has no mother or other dutiful family member to make the necessary social connections. Furthermore, in terms of the companionate [companionable] marriage that lies at the heart of the developing domestic ideal, Cathy no longer has much in common with Heathcliff: "And should I always be sitting with you. . . . What good do I get— What do you talk about? . . . It is no company at all, when people know nothing and say nothing." Edgar, at least, is "pleasant to be with." Nevertheless, Cathy's dissatisfaction in becoming the "lady of Thrushcross Grange" and her self-alienation in her new identity account not only for her unwonted [unusual] "seasons of gloom" after her marriage but also for her fervid distraction during her second illness.

The persistent bond between Cathy and Heathcliff dominates most cinematic adaptations and prompts critics to invoke the term *myth*. Eagleton suggests that what originally draws the two together is that neither can expect to inherit

property, unlike Hindley; but the fierce, adversarial, grave-defying attachment that the novel imagines seems to defeat any effort to account for it solely or primarily in social and material terms. Both Pauline Nestor and Patsy Stoneman have explored the novel's representation of Cathy and Heathcliff from a psychoanalytic perspective, as a fantasy about dissolving the boundary between self and other and thus returning to a time [of life] before ego and identity come into being. I find this reading not only illuminating in itself but also relevant to the social considerations I have been emphasizing here: it points to the nexus [link] of the psychical and the social, which are necessarily intertwined in subjective experience. Cathy's "I *am* Heathcliff" may be understood as an attempt to annul the distinctions of gender, race, and class that Hindley (standing in for the social world more generally) has enforced and from which identities are produced. Some members of the class may choose to regard Cathy's "mental illness" as no more than the self-imposed fit of a spoiled young woman, but others will take more seriously the social and psychical factors that have produced her condition.

Cathy and Heathcliff Are Products of Their Society

This point is important because students are sometimes hard-pressed to sympathize with either the elder Cathy or Heathcliff as individuals—a different matter from sympathizing with their longing to be together. A complex grasp of the novel simultaneously demands such sympathy and makes it difficult, not only because Nelly, by her own admission, is fond of neither but also because Heathcliff is brutal and Cathy is profoundly self-centered. Her "I *am* Heathcliff" may challenge "conventional notions of selfhood," as Nestor argues, but it does so by appropriating Heathcliff's self, as Von Sneidern's reading of his "complete submission to her will" suggests. One way of awakening some sympathy for Heathcliff is to ask

whether, and how, his account of the bond between him and Cathy might differ from the one Cathy presents to Nelly. Even Nelly is moved to take his part when Cathy tries to persuade herself that Heathcliff "does not know what being in love is."

Another way of getting students to sympathize with both characters is to consider the way their social situations, born of specific historical pressures, have contributed to their peculiar psychologies and their ways of coping with adversity. Among my students, a minority or working-class student often undertakes Heathcliff's defense on social grounds, speaking passionately about his status as an outsider and laying the charge of his brutality against his own brutal treatment. At such a point in the discussion, I link Heathcliff's remaking of himself during his absence to new possibilities for upward mobility, represented here as an opportunity for the oppressed to become the oppressor. Eagleton suggestively reads Heathcliff as the "indirect symbol of the aggressive industrial bourgeoisie of Emily Brontë's own time." As for Cathy, Heathcliff's arrival in the guise of a (self-made) gentleman perhaps makes her regret what originally seemed the only reasonable choice; at the same time, his presence returns Cathy to the terrifying yet desirable prospect of the effacement of the self's boundaries and tears from its psychical moorings her acquired social identity as the "lady of Thrushcross Grange." . . .

Does the Ending Suggest Class Harmony?

The ending of the novel, with young Catherine poised to marry the newly "civilized" Hareton and move back to Thrushcross Grange, works neatly into the related contexts of a changing social structure and the homogenizing of regional differences. Instructors can usefully put to students the questions that criticism has taken up in a variety of ways: Is the picture of cozy, genteel domesticity to be welcomed or regretted? Is the devastation of Joseph's productive currant and gooseberry bushes for an ornamental bed of Grange flowers a positive sign or an ominous one? Is the shutting up of Wuthering Heights and the planned removal to Thrushcross Grange a symbol of the disappearance of the yeomanry and the triumph of a more socially homogenized gentility? Or has the restoration of the old house to its "ancient stock," along with the Earnshaw appropriation of the Grange and its lands, reinvigorated a world ravaged by the rapacity [greed] of the "aggressive industrial bourgeoisie" in its new social alliance with land (the spiritual vacuity of which is suggested by Linton Heathcliff, the offspring of a Heathcliff and a Linton)? To frame the questions this way is to emphasize the novel's largely symbolic representation of social forces over the subjective dynamics of Heathcliff's obsession with the elder Cathy and his hope of becoming one with her, finally, in death. Their longing for each other is the recalcitrant [wayward] mythic remainder of *Wuthering Heights*, which resists being rationalized away in terms of contending social forces. Helping our students understand these forces should not prevent us from acknowledging the novel's enduring mythic power.

Wuthering Heights Depicts the Conflict Between Natural and Social Values

Richard Benvenuto

Richard Benvenuto was an associate professor of English at Michigan State University. He published numerous articles on Charlotte and Emily Brontë, Robert Browning, Ernest Dowson, George Gissing, and John Keats.

In this selection, Benvenuto explains that the central duality in Wuthering Heights *springs from the conflict between two families, the Lintons and the Earnshaws. Each has its own values and approaches to life: The Earnshaws are violent, passionate, and fundamentally uncivilized, while the Lintons are rational, formal, and conventional. Benvenuto maintains that the tension between members of these families represents the class conflict that raged in England during the Victorian era.*

Like [Emily] Brontë's poetry, *Wuthering Heights* anticipates twentieth-century literature—in its complex point of view, its violence, its use of dramatic scene instead of authorial comment or summary, its moral impartiality. It transcends its time as few other Victorian novels do, yet it has points of connection with them and with the literary traditions of the nineteenth century. Like most major novelists from [Charles] Dickens to [Thomas] Hardy, she was drawn to the figure of the orphan, and drew a composite orphan-symbol in Heathcliff and Hareton. She uses, in fact, a number of familiar literary conventions or themes. *Wuthering Heights* is a revenge story, in which Heathcliff, like the illegitimate Edmund in

[William Shakespeare's play] *King Lear*, plots to dispossess Hindley of the Heights, and almost brings havoc to all the Earnshaws and Lintons. Brontë read Gothic fiction, and her description of the Heights resembles that of typical Gothic mansions—mysterious, isolated dwellings, with dark passages and locked rooms, where one encounters ghostly horrors and the supernatural. Heathcliff's ancestry includes the Byronic hero [ideal but flawed; typical of Lord Byron's poetry] and possibly [John] Milton's Satan [a character in Milton's epic poem *Paradise Lost*]. Like them, Heathcliff is a dark, morose, violent man tormented by his fierce desire and his loss. Stories of an ill-fated love, in which one of the lovers dies and returns from the grave to haunt the other, occur in ballad and folk tale. . . .

Brontë Surpasses Her Literary Influences

But whatever Brontë may have recalled or used from her readings, *Wuthering Heights* is not a conventional or formula novel. It is the cosmic vision of an imagination that for years had turned mostly to its own symbols and myths and expressed itself in secret poems. And it is not so much the portrait of a given society, as an exposure of the principles of social existence—an epic comedy [in this sense, a narrative that ends happily], despite its violence, that moves from a state of division and war to union and peace. If *Wuthering Heights* is unique, it is not because Brontë did not share the concerns of other Victorians, but because she dealt with what was timeless and universal in them, and because her intensity and thoroughness took her past the limits her contemporaries had learned to accept. . . .

The Divided World of *Wuthering Heights*

Wuthering Heights portrays the universe in microcosm, and it is a massive, epical book, although by Victorian standards it is short and extremely compact. There are barely a dozen characters in it. Its entire world is framed by the Heights at one edge and the Grange at the other. Yet the two houses and their families represent and unleash fundamental forces of life. Together they give a total symbol of existence, while in their conflict they divide existence. This division produces a profound dualism [two opposing principles], different scales of value, different notions of the ingredients of identity. We see an instance of this duality when Cathy Linton tells Nelly of an argument with Linton Heathcliff about how best to spend a summer day. . . .

The issue goes beyond the question of enjoying a summer day to become a definition of heaven: the two have different visions of life at its most intense or perfect. Linton, the boy, identifies with traditionally female qualities of passivity and quiescence, whereas Cathy identifies with traditionally male qualities of activity and exertion.

Neither Cathy nor Linton goes as far as their respective parents, Catherine Earnshaw and Heathcliff, who reject the heaven of traditional Christianity for one which only they can identify and share. Catherine and Heathcliff belong to the Earnshaws and the Heights, whereas Cathy and Linton have been brought up as Lintons, and despite their argument, their division is smaller than that between the Earnshaws and the Lintons, the Heights and the Grange. The two houses split the whole of existence into opposite spheres that contend for mastery over the whole—either by refusing to recognize the reality of its opposite or by clashing against it. Unconscious, intensely subjective desires versus conscious, public standards; passion versus reason; energy versus restraint; the lawless and the law-abiding—it is such contraries as these, opposite and interdependent as darkness and light, that Emily Brontë evokes in the drama between the Earnshaws and the Lintons.

The Heights Is Uncivilized, the Grange Is Ordered

The Heights is outside the law, outside the codes and forms of restraint imposed by society and civilized values—at least after the introduction of Heathcliff, whom we can consider as an Earnshaw. The Earnshaws have no limit to their passions, but love and hate with equal intensity, as if gripped by a mono-mania [an obsession with a single idea] that will not allow compromise, that cannot heed the voice of reason or even self-preservation. Hindley's torment after the death of his wife, Frances, is as extreme and obliterating of all else as is Heathcliff's after the death of Catherine. And it is as savage . . . *Wuthering Heights* is a violent novel; the Heights is the home or incarnation of violence. At one point Hindley pushes a knife between Nelly's teeth. Hareton hangs a litter of pup-pies by a chair-back. Heathcliff kidnaps Cathy Linton and Nelly and imprisons them at the Heights. He tortures and beats his son into submission to his will, and when he no longer needs him, he indifferently lets Linton Heathcliff die. Catherine is wild and unrelenting and given to paroxysms of emotion that lead to her self-destruction. Between Heathcliff and Hindley there exists an unremitting, brutal state of war, and on the night of Catherine's funeral, the two enact a par-ticularly savage scene. Hindley has locked the Heights and waits for Heathcliff with a pistol that has a switch-blade knife in its barrel. He has vowed to kill him if Heathcliff attempts to enter the house. Heathcliff bursts open a window, and as the gun goes off the knife stabs into Hindley's wrist, causing him to faint. Heathcliff then grinds Hindley's head against the stones of the fireplace.

The Heights releases those forces that cannot be civilized, or that resist civilization—forces that spring from an almost obsessive will to power. As its opposite, Thrushcross Grange is a place of order, of submission to the rule of social law and convention. Life at the Grange is kept within bounds, just as the Grange—unlike the wild, exposed landscape of the Heights—exists as a well-planned park within the boundary of its walls. A pack of half-wild dogs prowls the recesses and dark corners of the Heights; at the Grange we find a library with rows of books. Old Mr. Linton and Edgar after him are magistrates or guardians of the law, and the Grange itself is subject to elaborate procedures of the law as enacted in Mr. Linton's will—whereas control of the Heights is a contest of power and chance between Heathcliff and Hindley. During her convalescence at the Grange, Catherine acquires a new and refined appearance and manners; it is her initiation from her original state of nature into society. Lockwood, the Londoner, used to the conventions and formal rules of society, has little difficulty adapting to life at the Grange; with its very different rules, the Heights is alien and threatening to him. Anything is possible at the Heights. There is a moral code and public sense of right and wrong at the Grange.

Values and Grief

The contrast between the two houses and families, between the self-willed violators of the law and the socially conscious guardians of the law, informs the entire narrative and is the structural principle of Brontë's vision. What is perceived as real, or as necessary to existence, she shows, changes from one house to the other, from the value system supplied only by the self to that of a community or a tradition. Both Hindley and Edgar lose their wives early in marriage, for instance, and react so differently as to cause Nelly to compare their moral characters.

> I used to ... perplex myself to explain satisfactorily why their conduct was so opposite in similar circumstances. They had both been fond husbands, and were both attached to their children; and I could not see how they shouldn't both have taken the same road, for good or evil. But, I thought in my mind, Hindley, with apparently the stronger head, has shown himself sadly the worse and the weaker man. When his ship struck, the captain abandoned his post; and the crew, instead of trying to save her, rushed into riot and confusion, leaving no hope for their luckless vessel. Lin-

Still from a 1939 film production of Wuthering Heights, *starring Merle Oberon (left) as Catherine, Laurence Olivier (second from left) as Heathcliff, and David Niven (right) as Edgar Linton.* © AP Photo/File.

ton, on the contrary, displayed the true courage of a loyal and faithful soul: he trusted God; and God comforted him. One hoped, and the other despaired: they chose their own lots, and were righteously doomed to endure them.

Edgar's personal tragedy does not shake his belief in a morally ordered universe or his trust in God. He controls his grief and lives afterwards as regularly and methodically as before. Hindley rages against God; Frances's death deprives him of his reasoning power—Nelly's metaphorical captain—and it makes the universe irrational and purposeless. Edgar, practicing traditional Christianity, can find comfort in his loss by submission to an absolute being that exists independently of himself. Hindley's loss is absolute: the self has no recourse or refuge in the void the loss has left. One can still seek for meaning in life; the other sees only meaninglessness.

There Is a Lack of Understanding Between the Grange and the Heights

In *Wuthering Heights*, there is an almost impenetrable barrier between the self-identity of each house and its identity for the other, and when one family uses its standards to perceive and measure the other, it does violence to the other. Heathcliff cannot be judged by the rules that prevail at the Grange, yet that is precisely what the Lintons do. His complexion is too dark, his manners too abrupt, for Heathcliff to appear to the Lintons as anything other than rude and boorish—a threat to their cherished values. At their first meeting, when Heathcliff is a boy, old Mr. Linton pronounces him a criminal, and suggests—perhaps half mockingly—that he should be hung at once, before his criminality emerges. Hareton appears as a dunce to Cathy, who disowns her cousinship with him. Someone who cannot restrict her self-expression to the forms of behavior her society approves of, like Catherine, must appear selfish, wild, and abandoned next to an Edgar Linton, which is the picture of Catherine consistently drawn by Nelly. Catherine and Heathcliff's insistence on a self that is bound only by its own rules can only seem destructive to the Lintons, who live by the social contract and the necessity for compromise and restraint. On the same basis, social compromise and restraint can only seem destructive to the Earnshaws, for whom the self is absolute. And in fact the Earnshaws make the same mistake as the Lintons, by judging the ways of the Grange according to what is valued at the Heights. Heathcliff scoffs at the idea that Edgar loves Catherine, because Edgar does not love in the only way Heathcliff can recognize: "If he loved with all the powers of his puny being, he couldn't love as much in eighty years as I could in a day." He goes on to denounce his wife, Isabella, as a "pitiful, slavish, mean-minded brach [female hound]." In an early scene, Hindley tells Edgar, after Heathcliff has thrown a dish of hot apple-sauce in his face, to "take the law into your own fists—it will give you an appetite!" Later, Catherine locks Heathcliff and Edgar in the Grange kitchen and, throwing the key into the fire, tells her husband to fight it out with Heathcliff, a much stronger man than the frail Edgar.

The Lintons understand only degrees of conformity to the law; the Earnshaws understand only degrees of self-assertion. This division in the world of *Wuthering Heights* persists and intensifies until the final union between Cathy and Hareton. Neither side has insight into the conditions of the other— Nelly, who understands and values only what is apparent to common sense, cannot see that Hindley is an alcoholic and compulsive neurotic: to her, he simply chose his lot. When Heathcliff tells her that he has done no injustice or anything else to repent of, and that he is in sight of his heaven, Nelly cannot comprehend him. She does not even attempt to understand Catherine's declaration, "I am Heathcliff," the meaning of which is incommunicable except to Catherine and Heathcliff. Neither side makes a genuine attempt to remove the barriers blocking communication. Linton Heathcliff mocks Hareton's Yorkshire accent. Heathcliff keeps the Heights locked and closed. Edgar forbids Cathy to go beyond the walls enclosing the Grange land.

Yet Cathy does pass the walls and is drawn to the Heights. Emily Brontë has divided the world into opposites that conflict with and antagonize each other, yet are attracted to each other: Isabella to Heathcliff, Heathcliff to the gentlemanly appearance of an Edgar Linton, Edgar and Catherine to each other, Hindley to Frances, an outsider with the social values of the Lintons. The attraction to an opposite identity suggests a potential in each for precisely that which is felt to be most foreign or alien to the self each is conscious of—or for what has been denied and forbidden them by the Heights or the Grange: social equality for Heathcliff, reckless adventure for Isabella. Her attraction to Heathcliff, of course, is shortlived, and he uses her only to further his plot against Edgar. But Isabella changes at the Heights, as a latent Earnshaw principle in her begins to emerge. Hindley shows her the gun with the knife attached to its barrel, and as Isabella describes the scene to Nelly, it is clear that her reaction surprises and even shocks her. "I surveyed the weapon inquisitively; a hideous notion struck me. How powerful I should be possessing such an instrument! I took it from his hand, and touched the blade. He looked astonished at the expression my face assumed during a brief second. It was not horror, it was covetousness." A Freudian [one who employs the theories of psychoanalyst Sigmund Freud] would almost certainly interpret the pistol as a sexual or phallic symbol; but we need not identify it as such to see that traits of her personality that Isabella suppressed at the Grange are coming to the surface at the Heights. It was her suppressed, secret self that was attracted to Heathcliff. In this and a number of other scenes, Brontë suggests that the two houses, although divided and opposed in their perceptions of each other, have an underlying unity. If in nothing else, they are the same in their violence. A more peaceful and positive union is possible only after an Earnshaw has accepted the Linton principle in him, and a Linton the Earnshaw in her, and the violence has been spent. . . .

The Combination of Heights and Grange Values Creates Unity

[The] primal condition of life for Brontë is a unity that overcomes or dissolves conflict and division. Both houses, not one or the other, comprise the microcosm of existence, and each house supplies for the other a fullness of life which alone it cannot have—completes its circumference of being to make one circle of life. Brontë's vision of this, of the relation of the two houses to each other, is best represented, I think, by the Taoist [an Eastern philosophy] symbol of Yang and Yin, the two principles which comprise the whole of existence.

One is light, active, masculine; the other is dark, passive, feminine. Yet the light is not all light, but contains darkness; and the darkness is not all dark, but contains light. The same can be said of Earnshaw and Linton, the Heights and the Grange. Members of the second generation, after the violence and polarization of the first, find their way to that truth.

Towards Unity of Being

As we know, Catherine dies halfway through the novel, and Brontë virtually begins the story again, using a second group of characters to reconstruct a triangle like that of the first generation, their parents. Cathy Linton takes the place of her mother. She is attracted to the fair appearance and cultivated manners of Linton Heathcliff, who, though he is the son of Heathcliff, resembles Edgar, from whom he will inherit the Grange. Linton Heathcliff is a skillfully drawn, grotesque figure in whom weakness produces ruthlessness. It is through his presence and death that the destructive elements of the first generation are purged, for he combines, as [twentieth-century literary scholar] David Cecil points out, all the negative traits of the first generation—Heathcliff's cruelty, the Lintons' cowardice—and thus the stronger, positive traits can descend to Hareton and Cathy. Hareton Earnshaw, the son of Heathcliff's oppressor, Hindley, takes on the role of Heathcliff, and is heir to the Heights. Cathy's progress from one to the other reverses the pattern set by her mother. Catherine went from the Heights and identification with Heathcliff to the Grange and marriage to Edgar. Cathy goes from the Grange to the Heights, from marriage to Linton to identification with Hareton. Also, as Catherine learns social manners at the Grange, Cathy becomes fierce and unrelenting at the Heights. Together, the two women encompass a cycle of identity, a full circle in which the three names Catherine carved on her window ledge come into being: Catherine Earnshaw, Catherine Linton, Catherine Heathcliff.

Moreover, the underlying unity of being that eludes the first generation appears more directly in the second, for these are crossbreeds, the joining of a Linton or an Earnshaw (Heathcliff) with its opposite. They are the combination, that is, of the forces that threw the first generation into conflict—the forces tending toward socialization and the law, the forces tending toward individuality and freedom. For life, as *Wuthering Heights* conceives it, to continue, the two forces must be brought from opposition to harmony, and the cycle begun by the division of the first Catherine complete itself in the wholeness of the second. . . .

The Ending Is Ambiguous

Wuthering Heights ends with its divisions healed and its conflicts over. Yet it ends ambiguously without putting a final limit to the meaning of what it has told, or to life's possibilities. We last "see" Heathcliff and Catherine through the eyes of a shepherd boy, who is frightened by their ghosts on the moors. The union of Heathcliff and Catherine takes place at the same time, or very nearly the same, as the union of Hareton and Cathy. On his last visit to the Heights, Lockwood sees them by one of the windows, where Cathy is teaching Hareton to read. Earnshaw restlessness in the ghosts and Linton domesticity persist, and these last scenes are a throwback to that early scene when Heathcliff and Catherine first wander across the moors to the Grange, where they see two children in the window. But then Edgar and Isabella were fighting, and Catherine and Heathcliff were attacked by the dog. In the peace that reigns now, the two pairs can follow their separate ways without interference or danger from each other—although Heathcliff and Catherine will become a part of their area's myth to haunt someone like Joseph.

Although their mystical marriage is their private heaven—or perhaps because it is—Brontë accomplishes more through the domestic marriage of Cathy and Hareton. They solve the triangular conflict of Edgar, Catherine, and Heathcliff. Cathy, as we saw, takes on the role of her mother. She bears her mother's name, has her mother's eyes and spirit, and completes the cycle begun by her mother. We can say, then, that she is the symbol of Catherine's presence. Hareton is the second Heathcliff; his upbringing has been a deliberate repetition of Heathcliff's. "Five minutes ago, Hareton seemed a personification of my youth," Heathcliff says. Hareton thinks of Heathcliff as his father and loves him as such. Thus, in the persons of Cathy and Hareton, we have the marriage of a second Catherine and a second Heathcliff. But Cathy is a Linton, and says herself that she is closest to her father. Except for her eyes, she resembles Edgar, and she has inherited his values, so that she is the symbol of his presence, too. Hareton is an Earnshaw and resembles, not his father, but Catherine, his aunt. Both Nelly and Heathcliff remark on Hareton's "startling likeness to Catherine." He is the symbol of her presence. In the persons of Hareton and Cathy, then, we have the marriage of a second Catherine and a second Edgar. Hareton = Catherine, and Hareton = Heathcliff; Cathy = Edgar, and Cathy = Catherine. This set of equations, admittedly tentative, would mean that the one marriage between Hareton and Cathy contains the two marriages that were not both possible in the first generation:

(Catherine) x (Edgar)

Hareton x Cathy

(Heathcliff) x (Catherine)

And even if Brontë did not intend that tight a unity, it is the impression of the living couple on Lockwood's mind that makes him wonder, when he is standing at the graves of the other three, "how any one could ever imagine unquiet slumbers for the sleepers in that quiet earth."

Heathcliff Symbolizes the Rise of Capitalism

Daniela Garofalo

Daniela Garofalo teaches English and gender studies at the University of Oklahoma.

In this viewpoint, Garofalo asserts that although many critics consider Heathcliff a rebel against tradition and capitalism, his history illustrates the roots of capitalism in society. Spurned by Catherine in favor of the more socially acceptable Edgar Linton, Heathcliff plots his revenge by accumulating possessions and land. His prosperity springs from his suffering and loss, Garofalo argues, just as in Victorian society capitalism grew from thwarted romance and death.

Heathcliff has been understood by influential critics as radically opposed to the world he inhabits, yet compelled to participate in it and mimic its capitalist acquisitiveness. [Literary critic] Terry Eagleton has argued that Heathcliff and Catherine's love constitutes "a revolutionary refusal of the given language of social roles and values." This relationship cannot be actualized in the real world, remaining an "unhistorical essence which fails to enter into concrete existence." For Eagleton, Heathcliff's true commitments lie with an "increasingly mythical realm of absolute personal value which capitalist social relations cancel. He embodies a passionate human protest against the marriage-market values of both Grange and Heights at the same time as he callously images those values in caricatured form." Whereas Eagleton sees Heathcliff's love as mythically opposed to the capitalist world he learns to monstrously inhabit by betraying his own revolu-

Daniela Garofalo, "Impossible Love and Commodity Culture in Emily Brontë's *Wuthering Heights*," *ELH*, vol. 75, no. 4, Winter 2008, pp. 823–829.

tionary commitment to love, I argue that Heathcliff's form of love is not a romantic [characteristic of an eighteenth-century literary movement that emphasized the imagination, emotions, and nature] opposition to capitalist culture, not a protest against an acquisitive economy. It offers rather an origin story that explains capitalism and lends it an aura of virility and excitement. Heathcliff is both a troubling embodiment of capitalist forces and their necessary support.

Heathcliff Becomes a Collector and a Consumer

On the face of it, as several critics have pointed out, Heathcliff appears to be outside of his time and place, the middle class world of the Heights and Grange. But in economic terms at least Heathcliff's apparent outsider status does not really signify an extreme alterity [alienation] but rather a certain type of immersion in the logic of industrial capitalism that privileges consumption associated with mourning and brutal profit-making. Heathcliff's productivity is the result of his lost love, but this loss generates a particularly Victorian kind of consumption stimulated by romance and by death.

Although Heathcliff rejects luxury culture by choosing to live at the rustic Heights, his rejection of Grange life does not signal a complete refusal of consumption. Rather, it indicates a different form of consumption that was fascinating to Victorians. Heathcliff is a collector. Although he imagines that Catherine is lost to him, he finds that she can, nonetheless, be partially attained through collection. For Heathcliff, the object of desire irradiates [spreads to] the entire world so that, once Catherine is dead, she becomes disembodied, everywhere and nowhere. Heathcliff tells Nelly,

> for what is not connected with her to me? and what does not recall her? I cannot look down to this floor, but her features are shaped on the flags! In every cloud, in every tree— filling the air at night, and caught by glimpses in every ob-

ject by day, I am surrounded with her image! The most ordinary faces of men and women—my own features— mock me with a resemblance. The entire world is a dreadful collection of memoranda that she did exist, and that I have lost her!

Catherine is everywhere present but in her presence recalls her irretrievable loss. The world for Heathcliff is "a dreadful collection." It is furthermore a collection of "memoranda that she did exist, and that I have lost her!" If the desire to collect is inspired in part by a desire for completing, for attaining the whole set, Heathcliff's collection reminds him at every step that it is a collection that memorializes loss and the impossibility of possession.

The Victorians Valued Collections

Collecting was an important activity for Victorians who had a "concern with aggregation—organizing individual things into groups of things" as is clear in "the domestic handbook, the emporium, the natural sciences, the public museum, statistics, genre painting, and the Victorian novel." Collecting, though, was a highly gendered activity. Collections by men tended to be scientific and "sought a sanctioned principle of order." Men classified objects of scientific interest replicating "the biological sciences' preoccupation with relations, introducing into classificatory structures a temporal dimension which privileged the historical and reproductive relations of organisms." Men's collections functioned in a public way, adding to cultural knowledge and finding a place in museums and public exhibits. Women's collections, on the other hand, "contributed nothing to public knowledge" and were connected only to "personal history." Women's collections were keepsakes, memoranda, often connected to loss, rather than classification, "an indulgent nostalgia." For [scholar] Tim Dolin, women's collections defy "our efforts to ascribe public meaning—some convention of narrative, commercial, or scientific order—to its displaced collection of objects."

In some ways, Heathcliff's collection of memoranda recalls women's collections, although his nostalgia is less "indulgent" and more obsessive. Heathcliff's kind of collecting is related to women through its concern with romantic love marked by loss. The keepsakes and memoranda memorialize loss, producing an erotic pleasure in loss itself. This is the kind of romantic love that has become the staple of the romance novel industry for which Heathcliff, as demon lover, remains a crucial figure. The publishing of series romance, probably the most lucrative genre in the publishing industry, speaks to the commercial power of romantic loss, of the refusal to give up the object of desire despite its unavailability. Victorian women's collections were frequently memoranda of this kind of desire as evidenced by the collecting of pressed flowers, love poems, and letters.

But this erotic desire for loss was not only specific to women. The Victorian period "gave rise to the mourning industry and the modern cult of tombs and cemeteries." [Literary scholar] Ingrid Geerken points out that the Victorian obsession with death produced an array of "mourning artifacts" that "either contained a lock of hair or were made with the hair of the dead." These objects were of such central interest in commodity culture that "an entire industry of hair working" arose which produced "objects as astonishing as the full tea set (made entirely of human hair) exhibited in the 1853 Crystal Palace Exposition."

Heathcliff's Collection Is a Shrine to Catherine

If for Dolin women's keepsake collections defy commercial logic, I would argue instead that they speak very pertinently and all the more seductively to that logic by appearing to be personal, individual, and outside of commercial relations. Heathcliff's obsession, which turns the world into a collection of Catherine memorabilia, replicates the logic of commodity culture by instantiating [making into a concrete object] a desire for the lost object. If everything reminds Heathcliff of Catherine, he, in fact, acquires everything in the novel that was connected to her: people, houses, land, and all the objects in her world. As [literary scholar] Steven Vine has argued, Heathcliff appropriates "to himself the powers and resources that earlier divided him from Catherine in an impossible dream of repossessing her, fruitlessly striving, by means of capitalist accumulation, to staunch the wound her loss has opened up in him." That he does not enjoy the pleasures of commodities, or consume luxury goods, only speaks to the fact that Heathcliff has a particular kind of relation to commodities; he collects them but he does not consume them for immediate gratification.

If Heathcliff's obsession with Catherine, which leads to this form of collecting, seems a mode of resistance to modernity, [literary scholar] Beth Torgerson reminds us that monomania [excessive single-mindedness] was considered a disease of civilization: "The term 'monomania' was first coined around 1810 by Jean-Etienne Esquirol, one of the founders of modern psychiatry." For Esquirol, monomania was a disease of "'advancing civilization'" or, to be precise, the disease characteristic of the "'rising bourgeoisie'" focused on "'self-fulfillment'" and social and economic advancement. Heathcliff's modern mania, in fact, follows the prescription for a productive society that political economists claimed was necessary.

As [literary critic] Catherine Gallagher has pointed out, British classical political economists insisted that "wealth accumulates not only if enjoyments are deferred but also if they never equal or surpass the desire for them. The non-pleasure/pleasure ratio would have to remain top heavy in the wealthy society." Gallagher traces a shift in political economy away from a concern with happiness. In 1836, [economist] Nassau Senior wrote that "the subject of the Political Economist is not Happiness but Wealth." Abandoning the concern with happiness was part of a shift in political economy away from ethics. Earlier radical thinkers, such as [poet] Percy [Bysshe] Shelley, had been "eudemonic or 'utilitarian' moralists, maintaining that the best social system, like the best individual action, is that which yields the greatest happiness to the greatest number." Eudemonism, or the concern with the happiness of society, "was a mainstay of radical reasoning . . . for it seemed to lead to the conclusion that political institutions should be democratized to reflect the interests, and therefore promote the happiness, of the majority." But if this was the emphasis of [revolutionary author] Thomas Paine, [political writer] William Godwin, Shelley, and [social reformer] Jeremy Bentham, later thinkers such as [economists] J.R. McCulloch and Senior insisted that "political economy could not be a science of happiness." A productive society needed to delay happiness or pleasure in order to produce wealth. Heathcliff resembles this model of productivity as a producer and accumulator of wealth who delays his pleasure or consummation.

Heathcliff Is Both Lover and Capitalist

There is, then, a more masculine dimension to Heathcliff's collection. Hardly a benign collection of scraps of personal history, Heathcliff's collection is the result of conquest, humiliation, and brutality. To collect is also to attempt to control the world; if the classificatory efforts of male collectors seem relatively innocuous, critics have pointed to how these scientific efforts lent themselves to a certain classification of the world that allowed for its conquest and control.

Heathcliff is both a romantic lover associated with a feminine form of collecting and a masculine type of the Victorian capitalist, dedicated to accumulation rather than consumption. In this way, Heathcliff encapsulates a Victorian logic of collection, a type of consumption motored by loss, lack, and mourning, that extends to both genders. Rather than repeating the historical association of consumption with women, the

Promotional poster for the 1939 film adaptation of Wuthering Heights. © CinemaPhoto/
Corbis.

novel represents collecting as a form of both masculine and feminine consumerism. Heathcliff androgynously represents the consumer desire of both male and female Victorians, speaking to how capitalism vampirically feeds on the most personal, intimate desires. The more desire is magnified and rendered strange, part of a world beyond human control and hence almost supernatural, the more useful and interesting it becomes for a culture of mundane consumption and production.

That Heathcliff's love is the motivating force of his capitalist enterprises speaks to the nineteenth century's traumatic encounter with an increasingly capitalist culture. [Literary scholar] Gordon Bigelow has argued that the confrontation throughout the century between romantic notions of subjectivity and the nascent [emerging] study of economics led to the formulation of a longstanding conception of the economic subject. Thinkers such as [romantic poet and critic] Samuel Taylor Coleridge and [satirical writer and historian] Thomas Carlyle blasted both the capitalist system and its perceived apologists among theorists of political economy. These critics saw the capitalist system as a betrayal of authentic selfhood, a subjectivity beyond the cash nexus [focus]. For them, political economists attempted to reduce human subjectivity to concerns of the marketplace, thus denying what was most crucial in human beings: romantic critics saw "poetry, philosophy, religion" as "distinct from commercial life. . . . Wealth was not life, and its pursuit was not the pursuit of truth." Ironically, though, it was precisely this notion of a sphere separate from economic concerns that eventually became incorporated into economic thought, marking the shift from classical to neoclassical economics with its primary emphasis on the consumer. William Stanley Jevons, the most influential neoclassical economist, understood the consumer as an agent of self-expression whose desire was made manifest in the purchase of commodities: "[T]he market gives evidence of human desire."

Like romantic thinkers who imagined the possibility of a subjectivity set apart from political and economic determinations, Jevons defined the consumer "as a kind of natural force, like gravity, which pushes and pulls social institutions into the forms which most accurately reflect it." If "the romantic reaction against capitalism posits a subject replete with sentimental attachments and aesthetic responses, which capitalism gradually perverts," it is precisely this subject that neoclassical economists borrow in order to justify capitalism as the expression of inner, private and intimate desire. For Bigelow, the "expressive theory of the romantic subject . . . corresponds exactly to the dominant theory of economic value which takes hold after the 1870s in England, where the desire of the individual economic agent [a consumer] is assumed to be inherent in the individual, an authentic indicator of selfhood, which finds its objective representation in the commodity."

Heathcliff's Obsession Leads to His Capitalism

I see Heathcliff functioning as an early literary example of this desiring agent whose most intimate truth is represented in both his consumption and production. Still connected to the classical economic concern with production and yet anticipating the neoclassical focus on the consumer, Heathcliff makes engagement with capitalism a form of personal self-expression. If, as critics have often stated, Heathcliff is the ultimate romantic subject, Bigelow suggests that Heathcliff's romantic associations only make him the ideal subject of a developing economic system.

These claims indicate that Heathcliff is not the anachronistic other of capitalism but that his desire is made to order for this new economy, which gains its luster from what seems to lie outside of capitalism. If from Lockwood's perspective Heathcliff is an interesting rustic obsessed with his one object, unable to consume a variety of dishes like the urban sophisticate, Heathcliff proves to be a far more modern figure than Lockwood might wish to believe: not a throwback to an older era but a modern capitalist, brutal, hard-headed and miserly, addicted to the accumulation of property both in the form of people and land. In this way he actually represents not the opposition to capitalism but a way of, as it were, being a capitalist and enjoying it too. Unadulterated by the excesses of consumption that cloy Lockwood's palate, Heathcliff represents those archetypal Victorian figures such as the captain of industry, the venture capitalist, or the imperialist.

Heathcliff offers the fantasy that beneath the effeminate consumer lies a masculine producer who can reassure us that sublime attachments are still possible in modern times, that modem subjects maintain attachments to objects of desire even beyond the grave. When Eagleton and others see Heathcliff's love as a sublime, if unrealizable, alternative to capitalist culture, they participate in this fantasy: the logical supplement of a culture that nostalgically indulges what it appears to deny.

Wuthering Heights Depicts a Marxist Struggle

Terry Eagleton

Terry Eagleton is a British literary critic and Distinguished Professor of English Literature at the University of Lancaster. Generally considered a Marxist literary critic, Eagleton has written more than forty books.

Catherine's choice of the gentlemanly Edgar Linton over the orphaned Heathcliff sets into motion a chain of events that dooms most members of the Linton and Earnshaw families to unhappiness and early death, according to Eagleton in this Marxist interpretation of Wuthering Heights. *Enraged by his rejection, Heathcliff crafts his revenge, transforming himself from oppressed to oppressor and from penniless orphan to capitalist landlord. In Eagleton's view Heathcliff's story symbolizes that of the industrial bourgeoisie of the Victorian era, who challenged the supremacy of the landed gentry.*

[Catherine's choice between Heathcliff and Edgar Linton] seems to me the pivotal event of the novel, the decisive catalyst of the tragedy: and if this is so, then the crux of *Wuthering Heights* must be conceded by even the most remorselessly mythological and mystical of critics to be a social one. In a crucial act of self-betrayal and bad faith, Catherine rejects Heathcliff as a suitor because he is socially inferior to Linton; and it is from this that the train of destruction follows. Heathcliff's own view of the option is not, of course, to be wholly credited: he is clearly wrong to think that Edgar 'is scarcely a degree-dearer [to Catherine] than her dog, or her horse'. Linton lacks spirit, but he is, as Nelly says, kind, ho-

Terry Eagleton, "*Wuthering Heights*," *Myths of Power: A Marxist Study of the Brontës*, 2nd ed. Houndmills, Basingstoke, Hampshire, and London: The Macmillan Press, 1988, pp. 101–106, 111–117. Reproduced by permission.

nourable and trustful, a loving husband to Catherine and utterly distraught at her loss. Even so, the perverse act of *mauvaise foi* [bad faith] by which Catherine trades her authentic selfhood for social privilege is rightly denounced by Heathcliff as spiritual suicide and murder:

> '*Why* did you betray your own heart, Cathy? I have not one word of comfort. You deserve this. You have killed yourself. Yes, you may kiss me, and cry; and ring out my kisses and tears: they'll blight you—they'll damn you. You loved me—then what *right* had you to leave me? What right—answer me—for the poor fancy you felt for Linton? Because misery and degradation, and death, and nothing that God or Satan could inflict would have parted us, *you*, of your own will, did it. I have not broken your heart—*you* have broken it: and in breaking it, you have broken mine.' . . .

Catherine's Failed Compromise Ends in Disaster

Catherine tries to lead two lives: she hopes to square authentic with social convention, running in harness [combining] an ontological [based on being and existence] commitment to Heathcliff with a phenomenal [known through the senses] relationship to Linton. . . .

Catherine's attempt to compromise unleashes the contradictions which will drive both her and Heathcliff to their deaths. One such contradiction lies in the relation between Heathcliff and the Earnshaw family. As a waif and orphan Heathcliff is inserted into the close-knit family structure as an alien; he emerges from that ambivalent domain of darkness which is the 'outside' of the tightly defined domestic system. That darkness is ambivalent because it is at once fearful and fertilising, as Heathcliff himself is both gift and threat. Earnshaw's first words about him make this clear: "'See here, wife! I was never so beaten with anything in my life: but you must e'en take it as a gift of God; though it's as dark almost as if it came from the devil.'" Stripped as he is of determinate [defined] social relations, of a given function within the family, Heathcliff's presence is radically gratuitous; the arbitrary, unmotivated event of his arrival at the Heights offers its inhabitants a chance to transcend the constrictions of their self-enclosed social structure and gather him in. Because Heathcliff's circumstances are so obscure he is available to be accepted or rejected simply for himself, laying claim to no status other than a human one. He is, of course, proletarian [lower-class] in appearance, but the obscurity of his origins also frees him of any exact social role; as Nelly Dean muses later, he might equally be a prince. He is ushered into the Heights for no good reason other than to be arbitrarily loved; and in this sense he is a touchstone of others' responses, a liberating force for Cathy and a stumbling-block for others. Nelly hates him at first, unable to transcend her bigotry against the new and non-related; she puts him on the landing like a dog, hoping he will be gone by morning. Earnshaw pets and favours him; and in doing so creates fresh inequalities in the family hierarchy which become the source of Hindley's hatred. As heir to the Heights, Hindley understandably feels his social role subverted by this irrational, unpredictable intrusion.

Heathcliff's Potential Freedom Is Oppressed

Catherine, who does not expect to inherit, responds spontaneously to Heathcliff's presence: and because this antagonises Hindley she becomes after Earnshaw's death a spiritual orphan as Heathcliff is a literal one. Both are allowed to run wild; both become the 'outside' of the domestic structure. Because his birth is unknown, Heathcliff is a purely atomised individual, free of generational ties in a novel where genealogical relations are crucial thematic and structural importance; and it is because he is an internal *émigré* [migrant] within the Heights that he can lay claim to a relationship of direct personal equality with Catherine who, as the daughter of the family, is the least economically integral member. Heathcliff offers Catherine a friendship which opens fresh possibilities of freedom within the internal system of the Heights; in a situation where social determinants are insistent freedom can mean only a relative independence of given blood-ties, of the settled, evolving, predictable structures of kinship. Whereas in [Emily Brontë's sister] Charlotte's fiction the severing or lapsing of such relations frees you for progress up the class-system, the freedom which Cathy achieves with Heathcliff takes her down that system, into consorting with a 'gypsy'. Yet 'down' is also 'outside', just as gypsy signifies 'lower class' but also asocial vagrant, classless natural life-form. As the eternal rocks beneath the woods, Heathcliff is both lowly and natural, enjoying the partial freedom from social pressures appropriate to those at the bottom of the class-structure. In loving Heathcliff, Catherine is taken outside the family and society into an opposing realm which can be adequately imaged only as 'Nature'.

The loving equality between Catherine and Heathcliff stands, then, as a paradigm [model] of human possibilities which reach beyond, and might ideally unlock, the tightly dominative system of the Heights. Yet at the same time Heathcliff's mere presence fiercely intensifies that system's harshness, twisting all the Earnshaw relationships into bitter antagonism. He unwittingly sharpens a violence endemic to the Heights—a violence which springs both from the hard exigencies [necessities] imposed by its struggle with the land, and from its social exclusiveness as a self-consciously ancient, respectable family. The violence which Heathcliff unwittingly triggers is turned against him: he is cast out by Hindley, culturally deprived, reduced to the status of farm-labourer. What Hindley does, in fact, is to invert the potential freedom symbolised by Heathcliff into a parody of itself, into the non-freedom of neglect. Heathcliff is robbed of liberty in two antithetical ways: exploited as a servant on the one hand, allowed to run wild on the other; and this contradiction is appropriate to childhood, which is a time of relative freedom from convention and yet, paradoxically, a phase of authoritarian repression. In this sense there is freedom for Heathcliff neither within society nor outside it; his two conditions are inverted mirror-images of one another. It is a contradiction which encapsulates a crucial truth about bourgeois [middle-class capitalist] society. If there is no genuine liberty on its 'inside'—Heathcliff is oppressed by work and the familial structure—neither is there more than a caricature of liberty on the 'outside', since the release of running wild is merely a function of cultural impoverishment. The friendship of Heathcliff and Cathy crystallises under the pressures of economic and cultural violence, so that the freedom it seems to signify ('half-savage and hardy, and free') is always the other face of oppression, always exists in its shadow. . . .

Heathcliff Exposes Conflicts at the Heights

Throughout *Wuthering Heights* labour and culture, bondage and freedom, Nature and artifice appear at once as each other's dialectical negations and as subtly matched, mutually reflective. Culture—gentility—is the opposite of labour for young Heathcliff and Hareton; but it is also a crucial economic weapon, as well as a product of work itself. The delicate spiritless Lintons in their crimson-carpeted drawing-room are radically severed from the labour which sustains them; gentility grows from the production of others, detaches itself from that work (as the Grange is separate from the Heights), and then comes to dominate the labour on which it is parasitic. In doing so, it becomes a form of self-bondage; if work is servitude, so in a subtler sense is civilisation. To some extent, these polarities are held together in the yeoman-farming structure of the Heights. Here labour and culture, freedom and necessity, Nature and society are roughly complementary. The Earn-shaws are gentlemen yet they work the land; they enjoy the freedom of being their own masters, but that freedom moves within the tough discipline of labour; and because the social unit of the Heights—the family—is both 'natural' (biological) and an economic system, it acts to some degree as a mediation between Nature and artifice, naturalising property relations and socialising blood-ties. Relationships in this isolated world are turbulently face-to-face, but they are also impersonally mediated through a working relation with Nature. This is not to share [literary critic] Mrs Q.D. Leavis's view of the Heights as 'a wholesome primitive and natural unit of a healthy society'; there does not, for instance, seem much that is wholesome about Joseph. Joseph incarnates a grimness inherent in conditions of economic exigency, where relationships must be tightly ordered and are easily warped into violence. One of *Wuthering Heights'* more notable achievements is ruthlessly to de-mystify the Victorian notion of the family as a pious, pacific space within social conflict. Even so, the Heights does pin together contradictions which the entry of Heathcliff will break open. Heathcliff disturbs the Heights because he is simply superfluous: he has no defined place within its biological and economic system. (He may well be Catherine's illegitimate half-brother, just as he may well have passed his two-year absence in Tunbridge Wells.) The superfluity he embodies is that of a sheerly human demand for recognition; but since there is no space for such surplus within the terse economy of the Heights, it proves destructive rather than creative in effect, straining and overloading already taut relationships. Heathcliff catalyses an aggression intrinsic to Heights society; that sound blow Hindley hands out to Catherine on the evening of Heathcliff's first appearance is slight but significant evidence against the case that conflict starts only with Heathcliff's arrival.

The effect of Heathcliff is to explode those conflicts into antagonisms which finally rip the place apart. . . .

Oppression Turns Heathcliff into a Harsh Capitalist

I take it that Heathcliff, up to the point at which Cathy rejects him, is in general an admirable character. His account of the Grange adventure, candid, satirical and self-aware as it is, might itself be enough to enforce this point; and we have in any case on the other side only the self-confessedly biased testimony of Nelly Dean. Even according to Nelly's grudging commentary, Heathcliff as a child is impressively patient and uncomplaining (although Nelly adds 'sullen' out of spite), and the heart-rending cry he raises when old Earnshaw dies is difficult to square with her implication that he felt no gratitude to his benefactor. He bears Hindley's vindictive treatment well, and tries pathetically to keep culturally abreast of Catherine despite it. The novel says quite explicitly that Hindley's systematic degradation of Heathcliff 'was enough to make a fiend of a saint'; and we should not therefore be surprised that what it does, more precisely, is to produce a pitiless capitalist landlord out of an oppressed child. Heathcliff the adult is in one sense an inversion, in another sense an organic outgrowth, of Heathcliff the child. Heathcliff the child was an isolated figure whose freedom from given genealogical ties offered, as I have argued, fresh possibilities of relationship; Heathcliff the adult is the atomic capitalist to whom relational bonds are nothing, whose individualism is now enslaving rather than liberating. The child knew the purely negative freedom of running wild; the adult, as a man vehemently pursuing ends progressively alien to him, knows only the delusory freedom of exploiting others. The point is that such freedom seems the only kind available in this society, once the relationship with Catherine has collapsed; the only mode of self-affirmation left to Heathcliff is that of oppression which, since it involves self-oppression, is no affirmation at all. Heathcliff is a self-tormentor, a man who is in hell because he can avenge himself on the system which has robbed him of his soul only by battling with it on its own hated terms. If as a child he was outside and inside that system simultaneously, wandering on the moors and working on the farm, he lives out a similar self-division as an adult, trapped in the grinding contradiction between a false social self and the true identity which lies with Catherine. The social self is false, not because Heathcliff is only apparently brutal—that he certainly is—but because it is contradictorily related to the authentic selfhood which is his passion for Catherine. He installs himself at the centre of conventional society, but with wholly negative and inimical [hostile] intent; his social role is a calculated self-contradiction, created first to further and then fiercely displace, his asocial passion for Catherine.

Heathcliff Is In Conflict with Both the Heights and the Grange

Heathcliff's social relation to both Heights and Grange is one of the most complex issues in the novel. Lockwood remarks that he looks too genteel for the Heights; and indeed, in so far as he represents the victory of capitalist property-dealing over the traditional yeoman economy of the Earnshaws, he is inevitably aligned with the world of the Grange. Heathcliff is a dynamic force which seeks to destroy the old yeoman settlement by dispossessing Hareton; yet he does this partly to revenge himself on the very Linton world whose weapons (property deals, arranged marriages) he deploys so efficiently. He does this, moreover, with a crude intensity which is a quality of the Heights world; his roughness and resilience link him culturally to *Wuthering Heights*, and he exploits those qualities to destroy both it and the Grange. He is, then, a force which springs out of the Heights yet subverts it, breaking beyond its constrictions into a new, voracious acquisitiveness.

His capitalist brutality is an extension as well as a negation of the Heights world he knew as a child; and to that extent there is continuity between his childhood and adult protests against Grange values, if not against Grange weapons. Heathcliff is subjectively a Heights figure opposing the Grange, and objectively a Grange figure undermining the Heights; he focuses acutely the contradictions between the two worlds. His rise to power symbolises at once the triumph of the oppressed over capitalism and the triumph of capitalism over the oppressed.

He is, indeed, contradiction incarnate—both progressive and outdated, at once caricature of and traditionalist protest against the agrarian capitalist forces of Thrushcross Grange. He harnesses those forces to worst the Grange, to beat it at its own game; but in doing so he parodies that property-system, operates against the Lintons with an unLinton-like explicitness and extremism. He behaves in this way because his 'soul' belongs not to that world but to Catherine; and in that sense his true commitment is an 'out-dated' one, to a past, increasingly mythical realm of absolute personal value which capitalist social relations cancel. He embodies a passionate human protest against the marriage-market values of both Grange and Heights at the same time as he callously images [mirrors] those values in caricatured form. Heathcliff exacts vengeance from that society precisely by extravagantly enacting its twisted priorities, becoming a darkly satirical commentary on conventional mores. If he is in one sense a progressive historical force, he belongs in another sense to the superseded world of the Heights, so that his death and the closing-up of the house seem logically related. In the end Heathcliff is defeated and the Heights restored to its rightful owner; yet at the same time the trends he epitomises triumph in the form of the Grange, to which Hareton and young Catherine move away. Hareton wins and loses the Heights simultaneously; dispossessed by Heathcliff, he repossesses the place only to be in that act assimilated by Thrushcross Grange. And if Hareton both wins and loses, then Heathcliff himself is both ousted and victorious. . . .

[There is] a real ambiguity in the novel. In one sense, the old values have triumphed over the ruptive [disruptive] usurper: Hareton has wrested back his birthright, and the qualities he symbolises, while preserving their authentic vigour, will be fertilised by the civilising grace which the Grange, in the form of young Catherine, can bring. Heathcliff's career appears from his perspective as a shattering but short-lived interlude, after which true balance may be slowly recovered. In a more obvious sense, however, the Grange has won: the Heights is shut up and Hareton will become the new squire. Heathcliff, then, has been the blunt instrument by which the remnants of the Earnshaw world have been transformed into a fully-fledged capitalist class—the historical medium whereby that world is at once annihilated and elevated to the Grange. Thrushcross values have entered into productive dialogue with rough material reality and, by virtue of this spiritual transfusion, ensured their continuing survival; the Grange comes to the Heights and gathers back to itself what the Heights can yield it. This is why it will not do to read the novel's conclusion as some neatly reciprocal symbolic alliance between the two universes, a symmetrical symbiosis of bourgeois realism and upper-class cultivation. Whatever unity the book finally establishes, it is certainly not symmetrical: in a victory for the progressive forces of agrarian capitalism, Hareton, last survivor of the traditional order, is smoothly incorporated into the Grange. . . .

Heathcliff Is Both Victim and Oppressor

We can now ask what these contradictions in the figure of Heathcliff actually amount to. It seems to me possible to decipher in the struggle between Heathcliff and the Grange an imaginatively transposed version of that contemporary conflict between bourgeoisie and landed gentry which I have argued is central to Charlotte's work. The relationship holds in no precise detail, since Heathcliff is not literally an industrial entrepreneur; but the double-edgedness of his relation with the Lintons, with its blend of antagonism and emulation, reproduces the complex structure of class-forces we found in Charlotte's fiction. Having mysteriously amassed capital outside agrarian society, Heathcliff forces his way into that society to expropriate [deprive of possessions and property rights] the expropriators; and in this sense his machinations reflect the behaviour of a contemporary bourgeois class increasingly successful in its penetration of landed property. He belongs fully to neither Heights nor Grange, opposing them both; he embodies a force which at once destroys the traditional Earnshaw settlement and effectively confronts the power of the squircarchy [landed gentry]. In his contradictory amalgam of 'Heights' and 'Grange', then, Heathcliff's career fleshes out a contemporary ideological dilemma which Charlotte also explores: the contradiction that the fortunes of the industrial bourgeoisie belong *economically* to an increasing extent with the landed gentry but that there can still exist between them, socially, culturally and personally, a profound hostility. If they are increasingly bound up objectively in a single power-bloc, there is still sharp subjective conflict between them. I take it that *Wuthering Heights*, like Charlotte's fiction, needs mythically to resolve this historical contradiction. If the exploitative adult Heathcliff belongs economically with the capitalist power of the Grange, he is culturally closer to the traditional world of the Heights; his contemptuous response to the Grange as a child, and later to Edgar, is of a piece with Joseph's scorn for the finicky Linton Heathcliff and the haughty young Catherine. If Heathcliff exploits Hareton culturally and economically, he nevertheless feels a certain rough-and-ready *rapport* with him. The contradiction Heathcliff embodies, then, is brought home in the fact that he combines Heights violence with Grange methods to gain power over both properties; and this means that while he is economically progressive he is culturally outdated. He represents a turbulent form of capitalist aggression which must historically be civilised—blended with spiritual values, as it will be in the case of his surrogate Hareton. The terms into which the novel casts this imperative are those of the need to refine, in the person of Hareton, the old yeoman class; but since Hareton's achievement of the Grange is an ironic consequence of Heathcliff's own activity, there is a sense in which it is the capitalist drive symbolised by Heathcliff which must submit to spiritual cultivation. . . .

In pitting himself against both yeomanry and large-scale agrarian capitalism, then, Heathcliff is an indirect symbol of the aggressive industrial bourgeoisie of Emily Brontë's own time, [a] social trend extrinsic [imposed from the outside] to both classes but implicated in their fortunes. The contradiction of the *novel* however, is that Heathcliff cannot represent at once an absolute metaphysical refusal of an inhuman society and a class which is intrinsically part of it. Heathcliff is both metaphysical hero, spiritually marooned from all material concern in his obsessional love for Catherine, and a skilful exploiter who cannily expropriates the wealth of others. . . .

The Heights Mythology

It seems clear that the novel's sympathies lie on balance with the Heights rather than the Grange. As [literary critic] Tom Winnifrith points out, the Heights is the more homely, egalitarian place; Lockwood's inability at the beginning of the book to work out its social relationships (is Hareton a servant or not?) marks a significant contrast with the Grange. (Lockwood is here a kind of surrogate reader: we too are forestalled from 'reading off' the relationships at first glance, since they are historically moulded and so only historically intelligible.) The passing of the Heights, then, is regretted: it lingers on in the ghostly myth of Heathcliff and Catherine as an unbanishable intimation of a world of hungering absolution askew to the civilised present. Winnifrith declares himself puzzled by Mrs Leavis's point that the action of Hareton and Catherine in replacing the Heights' currant-bushes with flowers symbolises the victory of capitalist over yeoman, but Mrs Leavis is surely right: flowers are a form of 'surplus value', redundant luxuries in the spare Heights world which can accommodate the superfluous neither in its horticulture nor in its social network. But though the novel mourns the death of Wuthering Heights, it invests deeply in the new life which struggles out of it. In so far as Heathcliff signifies a demonic capitalist drive, his defeat is obviously approved; in so far as his passing marks the demise of a life-form rougher but also richer than the Grange, his death symbolises the fleeing of absolute value over the horizon of history into the sealed realm of myth. That death, however tragic, is essential: the future lies with a fusion rather than a confrontation of interests between gentry and bourgeoisie.

Darwin's Theories Influenced *Wuthering Heights*

Barbara Munson Goff

Barbara Munson Goff was assistant dean of academic programs at Cook College, a part of Rutgers University in New Jersey.

Emily Brontë and Charles Darwin both lived in the nineteenth century and both thought deeply about the connection between the animal and human worlds, says Goff in the following viewpoint. There are similarities as well as differences in their beliefs. Keen observers of animal behavior, both came to believe in natural selection, with the stronger members of a species surviving. Goff contends, however, that whereas Darwin believed that natural selection improved the species, Brontë suggested the reverse.

[Naturalist Charles] Darwin and [Emily] Brontë [came] to very similar conclusions about human vis-a-vis animal "nature," at much the same time and "in the [same] air." Both were, more or less deliberately, building a case against the prevailing state of British biology and theology, dominated as both were by [Christian philosopher] William Paley's "Argument from Design" [used to prove the existence of a Creator], and, more or less concomitantly, against the social and psychological complacency that this natural theology had seemed to justify. . . . I argue that Brontë, like Darwin, utterly rejected the anthropocentrism [theory that humans are at the center of the universe] and notions of progress that had served natural theologians as both first and final cause; that Brontë, like Darwin, based her conclusions on observation and knowledge of the manipulations of "selection" on the part of animal breeders, as well as on close and relatively objective observa-

Barbara Munson Goff, "Between Natural Theology and Natural Selection: Breeding the Human Animal in *Wuthering Heights*," *Victorian Studies*, vol. 27, no. 4, Summer 1984, pp. 477–508. Copyright © 1984 by Indiana University Press. All rights reserved. Reproduced by permission.

tion of animal behavior; that Brontë, more aggressively than Darwin, had come to conclusions about the literal descent of Victorian man from his essential animal nature; that Brontë's conclusions, like Darwin's, grew out of a reverence for the pitiless economy of nature; that Brontë, unlike both Darwin and the natural theologians, was perfectly comfortable with a personal God who operated as ruthlessly as Darwin's "mechanism"; and that—to return this argument to the novel that plays out its propositions—*Wuthering Heights* represents this "God" of hers, this "mechanism," in the character of Heathcliff. . . .

Emily Brontë Understood Sheep-Breeding

Evolution had been, as we say, "in the air" since the 1830s, but that atmosphere was created largely by geologists and paleontologists. Little suggests that Emily Brontë had been influenced by that literature: Catherine's love for Heathcliff is, after all, "like the *eternal* rocks beneath" (italics mine). Nor is evolution per se (the development of new species over eons) the question or issue for Brontë, whose own sense of natural selection operates over both a shorter (since "1500") and a longer ("eternal") temporal framework. She is concerned only with the moral, social, psychological, and theological implications of natural science. Darwin himself had attempted, in the same years, to distinguish the issues by sorting his speculations and observations into notebooks on "transmutation" [biological changes] and "metaphysics" [the study of the fundamental nature of the world]. We do know that both Charlotte and Emily Brontë were avid students of natural history, delighting in such animal lore as the "Dogiana" columns of *Chambers's Edinburgh Journal*. Similarly anecdotal accounts of animal behavior also fed Darwin's notebooks and speculations. My own evidence suggests that Brontë knew, also, a great deal about the history and practice of sheep-breeding in Yorkshire and that these facts became as crucial to her understanding of human nature as they had to Darwin's theory of natural selection. Studying Brontë's work in the context of contemporary natural science confirms what had formerly been only an intuitive response to *Wuthering Heights*: that the novel is a hypothetical experiment in the breeding of human beings, conducted to suggest how the breed has been corrupted from its "native state" by the very civilization that the Lady Eastlakes [Victorian reviewers] arbitrate [judge authoritatively]. . . .

Anyone at all familiar with Emily Brontë's poetry and personality knows that she had no interest whatsoever in "society"—in any sense of the word. She did not go particularly out of her way for people, aside from her own family and servants, and was distant and diffident even with her sisters' friends. "All that I, a stranger, have been able to learn about her," [novelist and friend and biographer of Emily's sister Charlotte] Elizabeth Gaskell remarks, "has not tended to give either me, or my readers, a pleasant impression." Though Brontë's poetry reveals a private struggle to reconcile herself to her disappointment in human folly and weakness, she seems never to have altered her social behavior toward those she considered unjustifiably privileged, pampered, weak. An indefatigable worker herself, she clearly respected the industriousness of the working classes. Later biographers, therefore, came away with far better impressions by consulting family servants and local tradesmen, or their descendants. *Wuthering Heights* itself testifies to the close attention Brontë had paid the working people among whom she grew up, to her fondness for their "plain-speaking" and matter-of-fact vision of the ways of the world and of their supposed "betters." Brontë was schooled by them, and her sense of debt and admiration is, as [English critic Q.D.] Leavis suggests, a source for the sociological warp of the novel's fabric. . . .

Wuthering Heights Reflects a Religious Form of Natural Selection

Wuthering Heights [delivers] an emotional experience matched in rawness only by the *Lear* [William Shakespeare's play *King*

Lear] it so clearly resembles. As with *Lear*, we are presented with "unaccommodated man," "the thing itself," the "poor, bare, forked animal[s]" mankind becomes when bereft of artificial dominion over animal nature. As with *Lear*, it is equally difficult to locate an authoritative voice in the work, internal [within the novel] evidence continuously refuting all suggested formulations. Yet we do not come to the conclusion, as we can with *Lear*, that *Wuthering Heights* is simply nihilistic [a view that existence is senseless and void of moral truths]. Even [important eighteenth-century literary critic] Samuel Johnson would have approved of the novel's ending, for the virtuous seem finally to prosper. But what then is its creed, its argument, its moral?

I nominate an intuitive, religious version of the theory of natural selection, derived, as Darwin's was, from close observation of nature and a profound respect for its driving forces, the simultaneity of creation and destruction, the laws of conservation of matter and energy. *Wuthering Heights* shows these driving forces, embodied in Heathcliff, at work over three generations. Adaptation is, indeed, in evidence, but it is adaptation to an environment whose deterioration gathers momentum with the accommodations of civilization. Brontë differs from Darwin, however, in a significant respect: try as he might to avoid and deny it, Darwin could not help but suggest that evolution was progressive. Brontë's view is more traditionally orthodox, suggesting, literally, the *descent* of man, sin originating in our fall from animal nature. "Methodical selection," in man as in animals, has not improved the breed. . . .

Wuthering Heights Demonstrates the Power of Heredity

Were *Wuthering Heights* merely a romantic novel, it would have concluded where romantic novels, [prolific filmmaker] William Wyler's film version, and many readers' memories of it leave off: with Catherine and Heathcliff dying happily ever after. The sequel might have begun with the posthumous birth of the lonely, lovely, soon-to-be-landless daughter. But that was not Brontë's strategy. *Wuthering Heights* is, instead, a kind of botanical experiment, the grafting of a bourgeois romance of marriage and property onto a gothic romance of love and death. . . .

All of the characters, except Heathcliff, are varying mixtures of strength and weakness, cowardice and bravery. The traits they exhibit as children become exacerbated with age. Most of the characters, save Heathcliff, confess to a sense of being unable to help themselves when they behave badly, Catherine Earnshaw being the most extreme example. Her daughter, Cathy Linton, is a significant exception, for she always acts, even misbehaves, deliberately: the child con-artist develops into the only character sufficiently willful to stand up to Heathcliff. In short, Emily Brontë's "retrospective reconstruction of how things came to be as they are" speaks for a biological/psychological destiny, the irreversibility of human nature, regardless of whether her position rests on notions of humankind's fall or an individual's psychological endowment. *Wuthering Heights* is an hypothetical experiment in the expression of such parental sins or temperamental traits over several generations. . . .

Wuthering Heights Is an Example of Flawed Breeding

Wuthering Heights shows civilization, the process by which people "adapt external nature," as a reversal of the order of nature, making "the being weakest in natural defence" unnaturally strong and unnaturally brave. Edgar Linton, for example, can only bring himself to confront Heathcliff with the accommodation of "a brace of pistols" and a goon squad of peasants. Only the vicious taunting of his mate is sufficient stimulus to bring out the "animal" in him, and a power beyond his control forces him to go for Heathcliff's jugular. It is the moment when we most admire him; usually we are invited only to feel painfully sorry for him. Thrushcross Grange (a place where wealth, in this case the fruits of the labor of peasants, is collected, counted, and stored away) typifies this reversal of God's natural order. If Thrushcross Grange—it is difficult even to pronounce—is the heaven that so many of the characters tell us it is, then "heaven [does] not seem to be [Catherine's] home"—nor Emily Brontë's.

All sociological issues are, by this definition of Brontë's "creed," post-lapsarian [occurring after the fall of Biblical Adam and Eve], and her commentaries, however telling, merely symptomatic of a more profound vitiation [impairment] of the species, human beings having become the "artificial [men] of cities." Artificial wealth has made it possible for the inhabitants of Thrushcross Grange, including the tenant Lockwood, to cut themselves off from the land, do no work for a living, and act out a town scenario in the midst of rugged moors, which they keep out of sight and mind by the gardens, fences, and hedges of Thrushcross Park. The Grange allows for the proliferation of moral runts, whose very survival is made possible by peasants and servants. They sicken, even die, at the slightest provocation. Had they been born at Wuthering Heights, Hareton Earnshaw would have hung them by the chairback. Emily Brontë's contempt for them is exceeded only by Heathcliff's. *Wuthering Heights* is indeed a "retrospective reconstruction" of how humankind got into this sorry state, suggesting that the species has been weakened by poor breeding methods, hyperdomestication, and the hyper-"adaptation of external nature" to humanity's fallen nature. . . .

Emily Brontë Used Her Knowledge of Animal Breeding in *Wuthering Heights*

Brontë's vision of the natural order of things, as I have suggested, was very close to Darwin's, based, as it may have been, on the same sources—both written and observed—and the same sense of wonder in the beauty, economy, justice, and ap-

British naturalist Charles Darwin, whose theories of evolution and natural selection presented in the 1859 study On the Origin of Species subverted the prevailing notions of social and biological structure. Barbara Munson Goff argues that Wuthering Heights illustrates the moral, social, and psychological impact Darwin's theories had on Victorian society. © Louie Psihoyos/Science Faction/Corbis.

parent wisdom of "Nature," in Brontë's case, or "natural selection" in Darwin's. All of Brontë's works bespeak her belief in the "argument from design" and the identity of "Nature" with "God," but differ in her insistence on confronting the thorniest issues: cats with rats' tails hanging from their mouths, schoolgirls crushing caterpillars, the "nest of little skeletons" that drives Catherine to despair. The design of Brontë's universe is far more brutal than Paley's: these cases are not the exceptions, but the rule. And for both Darwin and Brontë, unnecessary cruelty was the distinct feature of human behavior. In nature, death and destruction on a massive scale are necessary for the proliferation of life and variety.

Darwin and Brontë shared interest in another line of inquiry, namely the vast body of practical knowledge and lore concerning the breeding of domestic animals, which had been rapidly developing since the middle of the eighteenth century. Indeed, Darwin opens his *Origin* [*of Species*] with an appeal to *prima facie* [apparent] evidence of species variation in the "methodical selection" conducted by breeders of animals.

The evidence that Emily Brontë had animal breeding in mind is not only remarkable in itself but reverses, also, most interpretations of the status of "civilization" in the novel. That the novel is literally about domestication—the dialectics of the two houses—is obvious on a first reading. Our difficulty in deciding which of the two houses harbors more perversity is itself a reflection of the reader's own social priorities. Sociological critics like Leavis, [Terry] Eagleton, and myself have little trouble deciding against Thrushcross Grange, but find ourselves in difficulty when it comes to arguing for Heathcliff and/or Wuthering Heights: there seems so much blatant cruelty and destructiveness on the premises. Considering that action, however, within the context of the realities of rural life—a context not available to most urbane reviewers and critics and, consequently, not brought to bear on the action— goes far toward explaining it as one of the hard facts of a harder way of life, the wisdom of which Brontë accepts. Comparing Brontë's vision of nature with Darwin's, finally, goes far toward elucidating the theories of both.

Take, for example, the constant routine of culling. People for whom animals are an economic system—and Lockwood has to be told that the nursing pointer [a dog] is "not kept for a pet"—do not sentimentalize or anthropomorphize [attribute humanlike characteristics to] them. Hareton's hanging the litter of puppies is not necessarily the act of gratuitous cruelty Isabella implies, especially if we recall the cruelty of our first glimpse of Edgar and herself, who "had nearly pulled [a little dog] in two between them." Heathcliff clearly does recall the incident, for he pointedly attempts to finish off the job of murder when he elopes with Isabella. Heathcliff's callousness is exhibited by all those whose own bodies are commodities: thus Nelly's contempt for the urchin Heathcliff and Zillah's for the puny Linton Heathcliff. They, like Catherine and Heathcliff, have no use for pampered, "petted things" of any species. . . .

The Poor Are More Fit for Survival

"Breeding" in the common parlance of the nineteenth century refers, of course, to the proper nurturance of "civilized" behavior. I have already suggested the ways in which Brontë implies that such "civilized," "artificial" behavior has weakened the breed of animals at Thrushcross Grange. A far more venal [obtainable using money or bribery] definition of breeding characterizes the notions of "bad breeding" that so frequently prevented marriage-for-love in the eighteenth and nineteenth centuries, thus indicating another way in which "methodical selection" had vitiated the upper-middle classes: superficial, invented standards, such as those applied to the sheep of Yorkshire, had not produced survivors. It is interesting to note, in this context, Nelly's use of the term: [for Cathy to] "sneer at [Hareton's] imperfect attempt [at reading] was very bad breeding." While Nelly seems to refer to "manners," she is in fact rebuking Cathy for a failure in human decency and a snobbishness about the Heights that Nelly has deplored through two generations of Lintons already. Such behavior is, indeed, part of Cathy's psychological endowment—"bad breeding."

Wuthering Heights selects for a different sort of animal, infinitely more rugged and surviving with little apparent variation for at least 300 years. Outsiders—except Heathcliff—do not hold up well there: the mistresses predecease their own offspring, the men and the peasants, who are virtually immortal. It takes years of willful dissipation for Hindley to kill himself off, and his father, like an animal or an American Indian, seems simply to know when life is draining out of him. Catherine has inherited both traits, her brother's self-destructiveness and her father's ability to die at will. Catherine and Hindley, furthermore, share a fatal attraction to "what is called 'the world.'" Hindley comes down from university, having "grown sparer, and lost his colour, and spoke and dressed quite differently"; he brings with him a "half-silly . . . rather thin but young, and fresh complexioned" wife, in the words of Nelly Dean. The ultimate cause of Hindley's self-destruction, and the proximate [immediate] cause of Edgar Linton's, is uxoriousness [submissiveness to his wife], an overdependence and overfondness that Catherine, in her better nature, calls being "like two babies, kissing and talking nonsense by the hour—fool's palaver that [Heathcliff and I] should be ashamed of."

Heathcliff is even more rugged than the native stock at the Heights, and Catherine has always recognized him as the neighborhood's prize stud. When he returns from "the world," though, his "cheeks were sallow . . . his manner was even dignified." When Heathcliff is thus groomed with wealth and power, Isabella Linton herself plumps (or more romantically, wastes) for him.

Heathcliff's pedigree is dubious and perhaps irrelevant, for the cities, as Emily Brontë well knows, are an environment in which more than one variety of "artificial man" survives. Thus the suggestion that Brontë is a proto-Social Darwinist misrepresents both. While Social Darwinism seemed to accommodate natural selection to natural theology and/or the idea of progress, it did so in order to justify the status quo of the ruling class: "fitness" most definitely included the ability to attain and maintain wealth. *Wuthering Heights*, however, suggests again and again that money instead selects for weakness, that it is the poor who are more "fit" for survival—or, at least, that those who do survive the harshness of their "artificially" brutal lives are virtually indestructible if feral. When Heathcliff disappears into "the world," he returns a success, by its standards, a rich man. Heathcliff thus possesses the ability to appropriate any and all forms of power: human kindness, animal ferocity, human abusiveness, the natural elements, money, land, and finally even death and the grave itself, as seen in his "Ghoul"-ish burial arrangements. Rather than Leavis's "plotting device," Heathcliff is a sort of first cause, a Prime Mover, a principle of creation and destruction in whose aura life is both conceived and terminated for the other characters in the novel. Heathcliff attains the status of a "mechanism" in Darwin's terminology, that which drives nature and thus human destiny, the natural selector. Only the equal ferocity of human willfulness—embodied here in Catherine—eludes him. Had Darwin himself been at less pains to eliminate irrelevant speculation on the attributes of Paley's watchmaker [an analogy for God] from the wonders of the watchworks, he might have identified this mechanism, as easily as Brontë herself seems to, with God. . . .

Wuthering Heights Contends Man Is Not the Center of the Universe

Wuthering Heights is about the colossal stupidity, arrogance, even impiety of anthropocentrism. So, also, is Darwin's *Origin of Species*: Darwin describes the denial of species variation [of his contemporaries] in the face of the obvious evidence of our own "methodical selection" as our "ignor[ance of] all general arguments, and refus[al] to sum up in [our] minds slight differences accumulated during many successive generations." Darwin's suggestion that "methodical selection" itself indicates not only arrogance, what we call today "playing God," but also ignorance is even more evident in his original term for the breeding of animals, "unconscious selection." The following passage (also from *Origin*) illustrates Darwin's own vision of humankind's reduction of nature to an "abnormal" state of artifice, unfit for survival—a view that closely matches Brontë's in its contempt for the civilized admiration of "external[s]" and for the human arrogance, ignorance, "unconscious[ness]" of the subtler design of nature:

> On the views here given of the all-important part which selection by man has played, it becomes at once obvious, how it is that our domestic races show adaptation in their structure or in their habits to man's wants or fancies. We can, I think, further understand the frequently abnormal character of our domestic races, and likewise their differences being so great in external characters and relatively so slight in internal parts or organs. Man can hardly select, or only with much difficulty, any deviation of structure excepting such as is externally visible; and indeed he rarely cares for what is internal. He can never act by selection, excepting on variations which are first given to him in some slight degree by nature.

Darwin is only more hopeful than Brontë that Nature/Justice/Heathcliff—"selection"—will always have the last word.

Wuthering Heights Demonstrates That Rebellion Against Class Conventions Can Succeed

Arnold Kettle

Arnold Kettle was a British Marxist literary critic, a lecturer in English literature at the University of Leeds, and the first professor of literature at Open University.

In the following selection, Kettle maintains that Wuthering Heights *is very much a product of the mid-nineteenth century. The two households it presents, Wuthering Heights and Thrushcross Grange, correspond to two classes in conflict in Victorian society, Kettle argues. Thrushcross Grange and its values stand for the ruling class that exploits the workers, who are represented in the novel by Heathcliff and his environment, Wuthering Heights. In Kettle's view, the novel is ultimately hopeful; even though Heathcliff dies, his rebellion against oppression has been vindicated by the developing relationship between Cathy and Hareton.*

*W*uthering Heights, like all the greatest works of art, is at once concrete and yet general, local and yet universal. Because so much nonsense has been written and spoken about the Brontës and because Emily in particular has been so often presented to us as a ghost-like figure surrounded entirely by endless moorland, cut off from anything so banal as human society, not of her time but of eternity, it is necessary to emphasize at the outset the local quality of the book.

Arnold Kettle, "Emily Brontë: *Wuthering Heights*," *An Introduction to the English Novel*, vol. 1, Basil Willey, ed. London: Hutchinson University Library, 1951, pp. 139–155. All rights reserved. Reproduced by permission of Taylor & Francis Books UK.

Wuthering Heights Is Not Abstract But Real

Wuthering Heights is about England in 1847. The people it reveals live not in a never-never land but in Yorkshire. Heathcliff was born not in the pages of [poet Lord] Byron, but in a Liverpool slum. The language of Nelly, Joseph and Hareton is the language of Yorkshire people. The story of *Wuthering Heights* is concerned not with love in the abstract but with the passions of living people, with property-ownership, the attraction of social comforts, the arrangement of marriages, the importance of education, the validity of religion, the relations of rich and poor.

There is nothing vague about this novel; the mists in it are the mists of the Yorkshire moors; if we speak of it as having an elemental quality it is because the very elements, the great forces of nature are evoked, which change so slowly that in the span of a human life they seem unchanging. But in this evocation there is nothing sloppy or uncontrolled. On the contrary the realization is intensely concrete: we seem to smell the kitchen of Wuthering Heights, to feel the force of the wind across the moors, to sense the very changes of the seasons. Such concreteness is achieved not by mistiness but by precision.

It is necessary to stress this point but not, of course, to force it to a false conclusion. The power and wonder of Brontë's novel does not lie in naturalistic description, nor in a detailed analysis of the hour-by-hour issues of social living. Her approach is, quite obviously, not the approach of [novelist] Jane Austen; it is much nearer to the approach of [Charles] Dickens. Indeed, *Wuthering Heights* is essentially the same kind of novel as [Dickens's] *Oliver Twist*. It is not a romance, not (despite the film bearing the same title) an escape from life to the wild moors and romantic lovers. It is certainly not a picaresque novel and it cannot adequately be described as a moral fable, though it has a strong, insistent pattern. But the pattern, like that of Dickens's novel, cannot be abstracted as a neat sentence: its germ is not an intellectualized idea or concept. . . .

The Narrators Reveal the Inadequacy of Common Sense

Wuthering Heights is a vision of what life in 1847 was like. Whether it can be described as a vision of what life as such— all life—is like is a question we will consider later. It is, for all its appearance of casualness and the complexity of its family relationships, a very well-constructed book, in which the technical problems of presentation have been most carefully thought out. The roles of the two narrators, Lockwood and Nelly Dean, are not casual. Their function (they are the two most 'normal' people in the book) is partly to keep the story close to the earth, to make it believable, partly to comment on it from a common-sense point of view and thereby to reveal in part the inadequacy of such common sense. They act as a kind of sieve to the story, sometimes a double sieve, which has the purpose not simply of separating off the chaff, but of making us aware of the difficulty of passing easy judgments. One is left always with the sense that the last word has not been said.

The narrators do not as a rule talk realistically, though sometimes Nelly's part is to slip into a Yorkshire dialect that 'places' what she is describing and counteracts any tendency (inherent in symbolic art) to the pretentious. At critical points in the narrative we are not conscious of their existence at all; there is no attempt at a limiting verisimilitude of speech. They do not impose themselves between us and the scene. But at other times their attitudes are important.

One of the subtleties of the book is the way these attitudes change and develop; Lockwood and Nelly, like us, learn from what they experience, though at first their limitations are made use of, as in the very first scene when the expectations of the conventional Lockwood are so completely shocked by what he finds at Wuthering Heights. He goes there, he the normal Victorian gentleman, expecting to find the normal Victorian middle-class family. And what he finds—a house seething with hatred, conflict, horror—is a shock to us, too. The attack on our complacency, moral, social and spiritual, has already begun.

Four Parts to the Catherine-Heathcliff Story

The centre and core of the book is the story of Catherine and Heathcliff. It is a story which has four stages. The first part, ending in the visit to Thrushcross Grange, tells of the establishing of a special relationship between Catherine and Heathcliff and of their common rebellion against Hindley and his régime in Wuthering Heights. In the second part is revealed Catherine's betrayal of Heathcliff, culminating in her death. The third part deals with Heathcliff's revenge, and the final section, shorter than the others, tells of the change that comes over Heathcliff and of his death. Even in the last two sections, after her death, the relationship with Catherine remains the dominant theme, underlying all else that occurs.

It is not easy to suggest with any precision the quality of feeling that binds Catherine and Heathcliff. It is not primarily a sexual relationship. Emily Brontë is not, as is sometimes suggested, afraid of sexual love; the scene at Catherine's death is proof enough that this is no platonic passion, yet to describe the attraction as sexual is surely quite inadequate. . . .

What is conveyed to us [and to Nelly when Catherine is about to marry Linton] is the sense of an affinity deeper than sexual attraction, something which it is not enough to describe as romantic love.

This affinity is forged in rebellion and, in order to grasp the concrete and unromantic nature of this book, it is necessary to recall the nature of that rebellion. Heathcliff, the waif from the Liverpool slums, is treated kindly by old Mr. Earn-shaw but insulted and degraded by Hindley. After his father's death Hindley reduces the boy to the status of a serf. "He drove him from their company to the servants, deprived him of the instructions of the curate, and insisted that he should labour out of doors instead; compelling him to do so as hard as any other hand on the farm." . . .

Heathcliff's Values Are Morally Superior

[Catherine and Heathcliff] are not vague romantic dreamers. Their rebellion is against the régime in which Hindley and his wife sit in fatuous [meaningless] comfort by the fire whilst they are relegated to the arch of the dresser and compelled for the good of their souls to read the *Broad Way to Destruction* under the tutelage of the canting hypocrite Joseph. It is a situation not confined, in the year 1847, to the more distant homesteads of the Yorkshire moors.

Against this degradation Catherine and Heathcliff rebel, hurling their pious books into the dog-kennel. And in their revolt they discover their deep and passionate need of each other. He, the outcast slummy, turns to the lively, spirited, fearless girl who alone offers him human understanding and comradeship. And she, born into the world of Wuthering Heights, senses that to achieve a full humanity, to be true to herself as a human being, she must associate herself totally with him in his rebellion against the tyranny of the Earnshaws and all that tyranny involves.

It is this rebellion that immediately, in this early section of the book, wins over our sympathy to Heathcliff. We know he is on the side of humanity and we are with him just as we are with Oliver Twist, and for much the same reasons. But whereas Oliver is presented with a sentimental passivity, which limits our concern, Heathcliff is active and intelligent and able to carry the positive values of human aspiration on his shoul-ders. He is a conscious rebel. And it is from his association in rebellion with Catherine that the particular quality of their relationship arises. It is the reason why each feels that a betrayal of what binds them together is in some obscure and mysterious way a betrayal of everything, of all that is most valuable in life and death.

Yet Catherine betrays Heathcliff and marries Edgar Linton, kidding herself that she can keep them both, and then discovering that in denying Heathcliff she has chosen death. The conflict here is, quite explicitly, a social one. Thrushcross Grange, embodying as it does the prettier, more comfortable side of bourgeois [capitalist, middle-class] life, seduces Catherine. She begins to despise Heathcliff's lack of 'culture.' He has no conversation, he does not brush his hair, he is dirty, whereas Edgar, besides being handsome, "will be rich and I shall like to be the greatest woman, of the neighbourhood, and I shall be proud of having such a husband." And so Heathcliff runs away and Catherine becomes mistress of Thrushcross Grange.

Heathcliff returns, adult and prosperous, and at once the social conflict is re-emphasized. . . .

And from the moment of Heathcliff's reappearance Catherine's attempts to reconcile herself to Thrushcross Grange are doomed. In their relationship now there is no tenderness, they trample on each other's nerves, madly try to destroy each other; but, once Heathcliff is near, Catherine can maintain no illusions about the Lintons. The two are united only in their contempt for the values of Thrushcross Grange. "There it is," Catherine taunts Edgar, speaking of her grave, "not among the Lintons, mind, under the chapel roof, but in the open air, with a headstone." The open air, nature, the moors are contrasted with the world of Thrushcross Grange. And the contempt for the Lintons is a *moral* contempt, not a jealous one. . . .

Heathcliff's Moral Force

We continue to sympathize with Heathcliff, even after his marriage with Isabella, because Emily Brontë convinces us that what Heathcliff stands for is morally superior to what the Lintons stand for. This is, it must be insisted, not a case of some mysterious 'emotional' power with which Heathcliff is charged. The emotion behind his denunciation of Edgar is *moral* emotion. The words "duty" and "humanity," "pity" and "charity" have precisely the kind of force [poet William] Blake gives such words in his poetry.

They are used not so much paradoxically as in a sense inverted but more profound than the conventional usage. Heathcliff speaks, apparently paradoxically, of Catherine's "frightful isolation," when to all appearances she is in Thrushcross Grange less isolated, more subject to care and society, than she could possibly be with him. But in truth Heathcliff's assertion is a paradox only to those who do not understand his meaning. What he is asserting with such intense emotional conviction that we, too, are convinced, is that what he stands for, the alternative life *he* has offered Catherine is more natural (the image of the oak enforces this), more social and more moral than the world of Thrushcross Grange. Most of those who criticize Heathcliff adversely (on the grounds that he is unbelievable, or that he is a neurotic creation, or that he is merely the Byronic satan-hero revived) fail to appreciate his significance because they fail to recognize this moral force. And as a rule they fail to recognize the moral force because they are themselves, consciously or not, of the Linton party.

The climax of this inversion by Heathcliff and Catherine of the common standards of bourgeois morality comes at the death of Catherine. To recognize the revolutionary force of this scene one has only to imagine what a different novelist might have made of it.

The stage is all set for a moment of conventional drama. Catherine is dying, Heathcliff appears out of the night. Two possibilities present themselves: either Catherine will at the last reject Heathcliff, the marriage vow will be vindicated and wickedness meet its reward; or true love will triumph and reconciliation proclaim the world well lost. It is hard to imagine that either possibility ever crossed Emily Brontë's mind, for either would destroy the pattern of her book, but her rejection of them is a measure of her moral and artistic power. For instead of its conventional potentialities the scene acquires an astonishing moral power. Heathcliff, confronted with the dying Catherine, is ruthless, morally ruthless: instead of easy comfort he offers her a brutal analysis of what she has done.

'You teach me now how cruel you've been—cruel and false. *Why* did you despise me? *Why* did you betray your own heart Cathy? I have not one word of comfort. You deserve this. You have killed yourself. Yes, you may kiss me, and cry: and wring out my kisses and tears: they'll blight you—they'll damn you. You loved me—then what *right* had you to leave me? What right—answer me—for the poor fancy you felt for Linton? Because misery and degradation, and death, and nothing that God or Satan could inflict would have parted us, *you*, of your own will, did it. I have not broken your heart—*you* have broken it; and in breaking it you have broken mine. So much the worse that I am strong. Do I want to live? What kind of living will it be when you—oh, God! would *you* like to live with your soul in the grave?'

A Relationship More Important than Death

It is one of the harshest passages in all literature, but it is also one of the most moving. For the brutality is not neurotic, nor sadistic, nor romantic. The Catherine-Heathcliff relationship, standing as it does for a humanity finer and more morally profound than the standards of the Lintons and Earnshaws has to undergo the kind of examination Heathcliff here brings to it. Anything less, anything which smudged or sweetened the issues involved, would be inadequate, unworthy. Heathcliff knows that nothing can save Catherine from death but that one thing alone can give her peace, a full and utterly honest understanding and acceptance of their relationship and what it implies. There is no hope in comfort or compromise. Any such weakness would debase them both and make a futile waste of their lives and death. For Heathcliff and Catherine, who reject the Lintons' chapel roof and the consolations of Christianity, know, too, that their relationship is more important than death.

In the section of the book that follows Catherine's death Heathcliff continues the revenge he has begun with his marriage to Isabella. It is the most peculiar section of the novel and the most difficult because the quality of Heathcliff's feeling is of a kind most of us find hard to comprehend. . . .

Heathcliff Undergoes a Conversion

Heathcliff retains our sympathy throughout this dreadful section of the book because instinctively we recognize a rough moral justice in what he has done to his oppressors and because, though he is inhuman, we understand *why* he is inhuman. Obviously we do not approve of what he does, but we understand it; the deep and complex issues behind his actions are revealed to us. We recognize that the very forces which drove him to rebellion for a higher freedom have themselves entrapped him in their own values and determined the nature of his revenge.

If *Wuthering Heights* were to stop at this point it would still be a great book, but a wholly sombre and depressing one. Man would be revealed as inevitably caught up in the meshes of his own creating; against the tragic horror of Heathcliff's appalling rebellion the limited but complacent world of Thrushcross Grange would seem a tempting haven and the novel would resolve itself into the false antithesis of Thrushcross Grange/Wuthering Heights, just as in *Oliver Twist* the real antithesis becomes sidetracked into the false one of

Brownlow/Fagin. But *Wuthering Heights*, a work of supreme and astonishing genius, does not stop here. We have not done with Heathcliff yet.

For at the moment of his horrible triumph a change begins to come over Heathcliff. . . .

Heathcliff Reclaims His Manhood

Once more the stage is set for a familiar scene, the conversion of the wicked who will in the final chapter turn from his wickedness. And once more the conventional must look again.

The change that comes over Heathcliff and the novel and leads us on to the wonderful, quiet, gentle, tentative evocation of nature in the final sentence, is a very subtle one. . . .

Cathy and Hareton are not in the novel an easy re-creation of Catherine and Heathcliff; they are, as [critic] Mr. [G.D.] Klingopulos remarks, different people, even lesser people, certainly people conceived on a less intense and passionate scale than the older lovers. But they do symbolize the continuity of life and human aspirations, and it is through them that Heathcliff comes to understand the hollowness of his triumph. It is when Hareton, who loves him, comes to Cathy's aid when he strikes her that the full meaning of his own relationship with Catherine comes back to him and he becomes aware that in the feeling between Cathy and Hareton there is something of the same quality. From the moment that Cathy and Hareton are drawn together as rebels the change begins. For now for the first time Heathcliff is confronted not with those who accept the values of Wuthering Heights and Thrushcross Grange but with those who share, however remotely, his own wild endeavours to hold his right. . . .

He has come to see the pointlessness of his fight to revenge himself on the world of power and property through its own values. Just as Catherine had to face the full moral horror of her betrayal of their love, he must face the full horror of his betrayal too. And once he has faced it he can die, not nobly or triumphantly, but at least as a man, leaving with Cathy and Hareton the possibility of carrying on the struggle he has begun, and in his death he will achieve again human dignity, "to be carried to the churchyard in the evening."

It is this re-achievement of manhood by Heathcliff, an understanding reached with no help from the world he despises, which, together with the developing relationship of Cathy and Hareton and the sense of the continuity of life in nature, gives to the last pages of *Wuthering Heights* a sense of positive and unsentimental hope. The Catherine-Heathcliff relationship has been vindicated. Life will go on and others will rebel against the oppressors. Nothing has been solved but much has been experienced. Lies, complacencies and errors, appalling errors, have been revealed. A veil has been drawn from the conventional face of bourgeois man; he has been revealed, through Heathcliff, without his mask. . . .

Wuthering Heights Is of Its Time and for All Time

It is very necessary to be reminded that just as the values of Wuthering Heights and Thrushcross Grange are not simply the values of *any* tyranny but specifically those of Victorian society, so is the rebellion of Heathcliff a particular rebellion, that of the worker physically and spiritually degraded by the conditions and relationships of this same society. That Heathcliff ceases to be one of the exploited is true, but it is also true that just in so far as he adopts (with a ruthlessness that frightens even the ruling class itself) the standards of the ruling class, so do the human values implicit in his early rebellion and in his love for Catherine vanish. All that is involved in the Catherine-Heathcliff relationship, all that it stands for in human needs and hopes, can be realized only through the active rebellion of the oppressed.

Wuthering Heights then is an expression in the imaginative terms of art of the stresses and tensions and conflicts, personal and spiritual, of nineteenth-century capitalist society. It is a novel without idealism, without false comforts, without any implication that power over their destinies rests outside the struggles and actions of human beings themselves. Its powerful evocation of nature, of moorland and storm, of the stars and the seasons is an essential part of its revelation of the very movement of life itself. The men and women of *Wuthering Heights* are not the prisoners of nature; they live in the world and strive to change it, sometimes successfully, always painfully, with almost infinite difficulty and error.

This unending struggle, of which the struggle to advance from class society to the higher humanity of a classless world is but an episode, is conveyed to us in *Wuthering Heights* precisely because the novel is conceived in actual, concrete, particular terms, because the quality of oppression revealed in the novel is not abstract but concrete, not vague but particular. And that is why Emily Brontë's novel is at the same time a statement about the life she knew, the life of Victorian England, and a statement about life as such. [English author] Virginia Woolf, writing about it, said:

> That gigantic ambition is to be felt throughout the novel, a struggle half thwarted but of superb conviction, to say something through the mouths of characters which is not merely 'I love' or 'I hate' but 'we, the whole human race' and 'You, the eternal powers . . .' the sentence remains unfinished.

I do not think it remains unfinished.

The Desire to Possess Property Causes Conflict in *Wuthering Heights*

Peter Miles

Peter Miles is an English literary critic and the editor of critical editions of Wuthering Heights *and Wilkie Collins's novel* The Woman in White.

According to this selection from Miles, Wuthering Heights *describes a patriarchal society where ownership of property is a birthright based on class and gender. Heathcliff begins the novel as a homeless waif with no family or breeding. The story of how he manipulates people to gain possession of property symbolizes the social unrest of the Victorian era, Miles asserts.*

Heathcliff enters the *story* of *Wuthering Heights* as a ragged child rescued from a 'houseless' existence. Yet, in the very first sentence, he enters the *text* as 'landlord.' Three chapters pass before Nelly's narrative disturbs what the reader initially gleans of Heathcliff's social identity with memories of his first arrival at the Heights. This return to the beginning of the story opens a chasm of information and interpretation stretching between the polarities of Heathcliff as adult 'landlord' and 'houseless' child—as someone lacking even the anomalous [irregular] social position later conferred on him with the name 'Heathcliff'. Bridging that chasm, that tantalising disruption of commonsense social and economic expectations, becomes a dynamic of *Wuthering Heights*. For the contemporary reader in particular, in the era of European revolution, this translation of Heathcliff needed explanation, embodying as it did

Peter Miles, "*Wuthering Heights*: Passion and Property," *Wuthering Heights*. Houndsmills, Basingstoke, Hampshire: Macmillan Education, 1990, pp. 53–55, 68–69, 74–80, 90–93. Reproduced by permission.

disturbing possibilities of breakdown in a social order familiarly guaranteed by watertight processes in the transmission of property within class and family.

The Nameless Man

As street-urchin Heathcliff barely enjoys being called 'someone'. Characters' recognition of his humanity is qualified by his categorisation as 'gipsy', as essentially outside and at war with a society of mutually reinforcing moral and economic relationships. The insult 'gipsy' carried a stigma in the eighteenth and early nineteenth centuries which was in proportion to that society's anchorage in the stabilities of land-ownership. Heathcliff's appearance in a rural economy, mouthing 'gibberish, that nobody could understand . . . as good as dumb', perceived as some rootless, perhaps racially distinct, linguistically separate, proletarian offspring of industrial Liverpool, is a manifold eruption of the outside into the centre.

Emily Brontë was writing *Wuthering Heights* during the Irish famine of 1845–6 when, [biographer of the Brontës Winifred] Gérin reports, 'the newspapers of the day were filled with reports of the Irish immigrants crowding the docks of Liverpool in search of food and dying in their hundreds in the cellars of the foul Liverpool tenements before help came, leaving an orphan population scouring the gutters'. The same commentator sees the lack of *explicit* connection between Heathcliff and such events as indicating Emily Brontë's determination 'to surround every phase of his life with mystery, to spread a supernatural aura about him from the first'. But how curious, then, to specify Liverpool—Ireland's gateway to England, situated just a long walk away from Wuthering Heights—for the Irish famine, appearing to Victorian eyes as one of the greatest calamities in world history, was part of what Liverpool necessarily connoted in the Hungry Forties. In 1845 the [British government's] Devon Commission began investigating the byzantine relationships between Irish landlords and tenants, a major factor in the peasantry's vulnerability to poverty and famine. In no other European country did so few landlords own so much land, nor were the tenants so oppressed, as a consequence of serial subtenancy [renting from renters]. Such was landlord-tenant conflict, aggravated by famine, that in the late 1840s the Home Secretary acted to repress crimes (principally murder) against 'every class and description of landowner' in Ireland. The Commission also warned of 'Irish ignorance, beggary, and disease, with all their contagion, physical and moral . . . intermingling with the British population' and of the difficulty of preventing 'the half-starved Irish peasantry from crossing the Channel, and seeking employment even at low-wages, and forming a pestiferous Irish quarter in every town and city'. Emily Brontë could easily have avoided any such associations by having Heathcliff found abandoned on those moors which have so fuelled 'mysterious' and 'supernatural' interpretations of the novel. As it is, as [critic Arnold] Kettle insisted, the Liverpool connection cannot be shaken off, nor can those refugees with whom the whole Brontë family, with their own Irish roots, would have inevitably felt connected, though doubtless problematically. One cannot insist that Heathcliff *is* Irish, or that landlord-tenant conflict is necessarily responsible for his condition; besides, historically he is a child of the 1760s rather than the 1840s: but for Brontë writing, and her earliest readers brooding on the making—and the threat—of Heathcliff, such associations were all too available. . . .

Even Heathcliff Is Impressed with the Changed Cathy

As young Heathcliff quickly learns, Cathy can enter the Grange (figuratively and literally) thanks to a deference to class (and in her case gender) on which we have seen Lockwood vainly depending: 'she was a young lady and they made a discrimination between her treatment and mine.' The values of the Grange are pleasingly aestheticised in those delightful surfaces of gold, silver, crimson and crystal which overlie the foundations of ownership, and which are not easily resisted: the Cathy who returns is a changed person; even the young Heathcliff sends forth this world with sighing, 'ah! it was beautiful!', though part of his future enterprise will be to subvert such values, to put gold 'to the use of paving stones' and polish tin 'to ape a service of silver.'

What certainly attracts Heathcliff, though, is property as personal space. Wuthering Heights is claustrophobic, not because of its relative size or inferiority of furnishing, but because of the oppressive presence of selfish authority—Hindley and Frances laughing and drinking before the fire, while the children read sermons and learn 'Scripture names' under Joseph's tutelage. Heathcliff finds Edgar and Isabella foolish in not appreciating freedom within a property space. . . .

Admitted to the Grange, Cathy succumbs to the graces of an environment displaying orthodox values in visual style. She is caused to recognise a cultural gulf between her conformist self and Heathcliff, between her potential destiny and his. But Heathcliff also falls towards conformism. He watches the new ladylike Cathy with 'shame and pride.' If he could reject the Thrushcross Grange of Edgar and Isabella with exuberance, only augmenting his sense of his own worth, he cannot so easily dismiss the Grange-formed Cathy. . . .

Patriarchy and Its Anxieties

Heathcliff's departure is triggered by more than his hearing of Cathy's acceptance of Edgar in marriage. The episode is highly theatrical, with Cathy unaware of Heathcliff listening or of his leaving at a crucial transition in her remarks—just as she declares that 'it would degrade me to marry Heathcliff now,' but also in the very breath before she adds that he will never know how much she loves him. Heathcliff has gone when Cathy indignantly asserts that marrying Edgar will not entail separation from Heathcliff; he has gone when she explains that if she and Heathcliff married they would be beggars, and that her best motive for marrying Edgar is her intention of using her position to help Heathcliff rise and escape Hindley's power. Significantly, Heathcliff does remain after she has explained that she loves Edgar 'because he will be rich, and I shall like to be the greatest woman of the neighbourhood, and I shall be proud of having such a husband.' However, her explaining how Hindley's actions have influenced her decision is crucial:

> I've no more business to marry Edgar Linton than I have to be in heaven; and if the wicked man in there had not brought Heathcliff so low, I shouldn't have thought of it.

Traditionally critics have emphasised the first part of this remark; rarely the second. Heathcliff's agony hinges on the role of his old enemy Hindley's actions. What the drama dictates that Heathcliff *does not* hear, intensifies the cruelty of the explanation he does hear. He leaves having had his dream of revenge upon Hindley ludicrously undercut by his 'good turn' in saving Hareton. He leaves knowing that pre-empting Hindley's persecution by cultivating a self-willed 'impression of inward and outward repulsiveness' has utterly misfired, transforming him in the new Cathy's eyes from the obvious prospect as a husband to an impossible one. But he may also be understood as leaving in search of a common remedy to his various frustrations: revenge on Hindley may not be separate from the problem of his own relation to society and its benefits, or from the now central issue of retrieving his relationship with Cathy. When he returns he has cultivated differences in himself to those specific ends. To Cathy he will say, 'I struggled only for you'—but that is to struggle with his whole condition of exclusion.

Having once been driven to and beyond the margins of community, Heathcliff's return becomes a second arrival, reworking on altered terms those collisions with property-culture in which his relationship with Cathy has become so deeply enmeshed. . . .

Heathcliff's Game of Property Acquisition

Heathcliff's paying Hindley liberal rent for lodging at the Heights initially seems ironic at Heathcliff's expense. But this is the beginning of Heathcliff's gambling his way to becoming mortgagee of the Heights, reversing the ironies as Hindley commits the traditional cardinal sin of the landowner—borrowing money against land. Hindley is thus eventually dispossessed of that very property which had empowered him to engineer the young Heathcliff's exclusion. It is more sweet a revenge than Heathcliff's initial intention of glimpsing Cathy once more and then simply killing Hindley and himself, and more than a personal revenge. Joseph's diction (which denotes individuals in terms of family relationships) intimates that Heathcliff is undermining the structures of family and inheritance themselves: 'I'course, he tells Dame Catherine hah hor father's goold runs intuh his pocket, and her father's son gallops dahn t'Broad road, while he flees afore to oppen t'pikes?'

Seeking revenge, but with no single plan, Heathcliff becomes a chess-player developing different areas of the board. Advancing boldly, he is careful to observe the rules of the society he is set on dismantling. Isabella speaks of his 'diabolical prudence'—and Heathcliff congratulates himself on keeping 'strictly within the limits of the law'.

Isabella's infatuation presents another property as prize— one he considers pursuable without harming Cathy's interests, for engineering his possession of Thrushcross Grange could only result in Cathy enjoying the property more fully through him than she does as Edgar's wife. (By contrast, Heathcliff refuses Isabella any part in ownership at the Heights.)

Heathcliff Compares Relationships to Homes

The elopement also highlights his argument with Cathy. Cathy and Heathcliff's antagonism, co-existing with their love, receives little explicit expression until Heathcliff contrives to see

EJECTMENT OF IRISH TENANTRY.

THE EJECTMENT.

Illustration of Irish tenants being forcibly evicted during the Great Famine (1845–1849). Peter Miles argues that Heathcliff represents English fears over the influx of Irish immigrants during the "Hungry Forties." © Illustrated London News/Stringer/Getty Images.

Cathy in her illness: '*Why* did you despise me? *Why* did you betray your own heart, Cathy?' Cathy's marriage constitutes the greatest barrier between them, and her acceptance of that marriage, which Heathcliff frustratedly respects, makes the barrier self-enforced and to that extent the more frustrating. Heathcliff's reproach is evident when he counters Cathy's suggestion that he has not thought of her during his absence with the rejoinder that her marriage implies she has thought of him much less. Reproach lies in his bitter rejection of Cathy's right to intervene in his courting Isabella, seeing that Cathy has already spurned him as a husband. However, Cathy's measured willingness actually to contemplate Isabella and Heathcliff's marriage provokes his strongest words:

> Having levelled my palace, don't erect a hovel and complacently admire your own charity in giving me that for a home. If I imagined you really wished me to marry Isabella, I'd cut my throat!

Laying siege to the Heights, and angling for some purchase on Thrushcross Grange, Heathcliff's actions and metaphors here interlock: Cathy's marriage has destroyed his dream of a 'palace' of fulfilled love; seriously to be offered Isabella as a wife by Cathy is to be offered a 'hovel' for that promised palace, to be patronised emotionally in a way which echoes the economic patronage of an owning class's charity.

Marrying Isabella also cold-bloodedly prostitutes that institution of marriage which has separated him from Cathy, creating through the sister a black parody of Cathy's marriage to the brother, a self-mutilation perversely designed to impress Cathy with its painfulness. Heathcliff may not respond immediately to Cathy's insensitive prediction of her bearing Edgar half-a-dozen sons, but there is a bitter riposte in Heathcliff's later telling Nelly that he has 'avoided, up to this period, giving [his wife Isabella] the slightest right to claim a separation': Isabella's tears on 'the very morrow of our wedding,' together with her questions and laboured reticences [silences] in her letter to Nelly, indicate that Heathcliff's care for the completeness of his travesty [charade] has only spurred him on to its sexual consummation.

Property Becomes a Tool of Revenge

In the later days of his plotting Heathcliff speaks far more openly about his purposes to Nelly:

> 'My son is prospective owner of your place, and I should not wish him to die till I was certain of being his successor. Besides, he's *mine*, and I want the triumph of seeing *my* descendant fairly lord of their estates; my child hiring their children, to till their father's lands for wages—That is the sole consideration which can make me endure the whelp.'

His forcibly pressurising Catherine and Linton into marriage further exemplifies his determination to transform marriage and inheritance from instruments of his exclusion into the tools of his revenge. Yet as symmetry of revenge forms under his hands and through the years, Heathcliff risks becoming the arch-defender of patriarchy. He has deconstructed and subverted marriage and inheritance as foundations of property ownership, yet drives towards a grotesque mimicry and extension rather than alteration of the systems he attacks, at a cost that includes the distortion of others and of himself and his son—who *is* his own son as well as a Linton. Being prepared to risk condemning the future to experiencing Linton as landlord—a manufactured monster of greed with only a poisoned appreciation of what might link man and wife, child and parent—constitutes a terrible legacy.

After Edgar's death, Heathcliff enters the Grange with 'no ceremony of knocking, or announcing his name; he was master, and availed himself of the master's privilege to walk straight in'. The nameless man has trodden a spiral—has left behind the namelessness of exclusion and even the inhibiting paradoxes of his acquired name, and through the power of possession has at last entered into a new namelessness, that of the master who does not require to be announced. With Linton's death Heathcliff sweeps every last remaining chip on the table into his lap. There remains his persecution of the dispossessed, Hareton and Catherine, as proxy victims, but this attenuated phase of his revenge falters. Having followed through his revenge on those most closely involved with him, on Earnshaws and Lintons, on Hindley, on Edgar, on Isabella—and arguably even on Cathy, he visits the sins of the father on the children; and in doing so the revenger in one generation becomes the tyrant of another. . . .

Literature's Social and Political Power

In Hareton and Catherine's story, the social perspective is in higher relief, and problematically so for the reader without any such perspective on Heathcliff and Cathy. As [critic Irving] Buchen indicates, if Heathcliff and Cathy's story is viewed as 'a typical romantic novel' then Hareton and Catherine's is bound to appear 'a respectable Victorian novel', thus producing 'Brontë the schizophrenic novelist.'

Heathcliff's movement from persecuting Hareton and Catherine to becoming preoccupied with rejoining Cathy is accelerated when he finds Catherine teaching Hareton to read a book she has given him:

> 'It is a poor conclusion, is it not?' he observed, having brooded a while on the scene he had just witnessed. 'An absurd termination to my violent exertions?'

As Hindley confirmed Heathcliff's exclusion from the owning class by cultural degradation, so Heathcliff has used it in revenge against Hareton, and even against Catherine. He succeeds to the extent that Hareton's illiteracy divides him from Catherine at the moment when she and Linton are actually bonding through the giving and sharing of books. Characters are seen in differing relations to books. Edgar (at one point to Cathy's fury) has his library; Heathcliff gives up book-learning in his adolescence. Lockwood tries to bar the dream-Cathy's entry with books. Catherine and Joseph threaten each other's library—though Joseph's extends little beyond the Bible on which he counts his money and the tracts with which he has made others' lives a misery. In this context, Catherine mocks Joseph's superstition very pointedly by pretending that one of hers is a book of spells. That Catherine is able to protect her own literacy at the Heights, and then resocialise Hareton through literacy, constitutes a powerful undermining of Heathcliff's strategies. This shared literacy becomes the central motif of the new Wuthering Heights.

In the nineteenth century literacy could appear as the key to resolving class problems. A burgeoning urban and industrial working class threatened the dominant classes with actual and potential claims upon political power and cultural institutions. The spread of literacy among working people aided the growth of class-consciousness, so management of that literacy from above was essential for the dominant classes. 'Educating our masters', ensuring that literacy involved a sharing of dominant values among the newly literate rather than an oppositional culture, became the project. The manipulative edge of this process, however, was masked both by the sincerity of motives among the reformers involved and by the fact of literacy undeniably bringing reward to the newly literate. What was read, what values absorbed with what concessions, could appear much less important than self-improvement itself. Managed literacy offered a softening of class division without a radical alteration of those divisions. The topic is touched on by many nineteenth-century novelists, and Emily Brontë's use of it is the less surprising in that while her father was educated at Cambridge, illiteracy lay in the Brontës' recent past and perhaps still in their Irish present. (It was Emily's father who first fixed the family name as 'Brontë', as opposed to the previous variations of Prunty, Brunty and Branty.)

The Uniting of Properties

Catherine turns Hareton into a potential husband, sharing with him her culture and then property in the form of the combined estates of Wuthering Heights and Thrushcross Grange. Marriage will now be a healing of Earnshaws and Lintons, and a model of cross-class reconciliation in classic nineteenth-century terms, replacing the conflict of Heathcliff's generation with a new deal. The sensitive negotiation and mutual understanding of Catherine and Hareton overcomes snobbery on the one side, and suspicion on the other. Their marriage is significantly delayed beyond the end of the novel, arranged for the 'New Year', a new era when passion and property will be united in culturally reconciled lovers. Wish-fulfilment is in the air: Wuthering Heights becomes surprisingly akin to a Victorian dolls' house, doors and windows open rather than bolted, vegetable plots replaced by flower gardens, its porridge dotted with primroses—a wendy-house [children's playhouse] free from oppressive authority (though with Nelly in an acceptable role as the parental servant). Although this ending attempts a social resolution of a social problem, it satisfies formal demands more than it solves the problems of class, gender and property, of human emotion and human aspiration which the novel displays. What Catherine and Hareton's future life at the Grange will be like is invisible to an assessing reader. Hareton, though in a gipsy condition, and in situations often echoing Heathcliff's, *is* still the last of the Earnshaws, the heir whose name is inscribed in stone. *His* is the fairy-tale ending Nelly once promised Heathcliff; but, a mere crypto-gipsy [unacknowledged as a gipsy] in status and personality, Hareton only has to be *restored* to his estates. To solve Hareton's problems is not to solve Heathcliff's retrospectively.

Wuthering Heights presents property as the condition ensuring that every man's hand is effectively against his neighbour; it extends one of Emily's formulations of the law of nature into an assessment of the hidden violence of property-culture: 'life exists on a principle of destruction; every creature must be the relentless instrument of death to the others, or himself cease to live.' It is Heathcliff and Cathy who expose that mechanism. And if it is objected that in her essay 'The Butterfly' Emily moved beyond such a view of nature to another, more happy and theologically conformist perspective on natural harmony, one may stress, beyond Heathcliff, the story of Hareton and Catherine.

Brontë is not a schizophrenic novelist torn between romance and social analysis: the social perspective is there in the story of the nameless man and the divided woman—and, if it is anywhere, romance is perhaps best detected in the wishful aspects of the treatment of Hareton and Catherine. Yet Catherine's strategy was a way forward, and one which the nineteenth century strove to take.

Servants in *Wuthering Heights* Have Power Over Their Masters

Graeme Tytler

Graeme Tytler is a literary critic and the author of Physiognomy in the European Novel: Faces and Fortunes.

In the following viewpoint, Tytler observes that Wuthering Heights *is unusual because of the prominent role the novel's servants play. They are critical of their masters, sometimes dominate them, and on occasion change the course of their masters' lives.*

*W*uthering Heights is exceptional among great works of fiction for its comprehensive delineation of the relationship between masters and servants. Such relationships constitute a prominent aspect of an essentially hierarchical, class-conscious community in late eighteenth-century England, reflecting in some measure the social differences between the landed gentry and the yeomanry [minor landowners] through the two households depicted in rural Yorkshire. Whether or not Emily Brontë's masters and servants reflect the England of, say, the 1830s and 1840s rather better than the England of the late eighteenth century, is perhaps a question that might well be asked, although it is one that appears to have been scarcely raised by any Brontë scholar hitherto. There is, nevertheless, a certain timelessness about the author's treatment of this subject, partly because it shows little of the perfunctoriness [superficiality] that generally colours relations between masters and servants in nineteenth-century fiction.

Graeme Tytler, "Masters and Servants in *Wuthering Heights*," *Brontë Studies: The Journal of the Brontë Society*, vol. 33, no. 1, March 2008, pp. 44–52. Copyright © 2008 by Maney Publishing. All rights reserved. Reproduced by permission.

This may be noted, for example, through the ways in which the characters portrayed as masters or mistresses tell us something about themselves by the uses or abuses of the power they have over others. And though it is plain from the narrative that the servants of both households, so long as they remain, or wish to remain, in service, are ultimately bound to submit to their employers, it is just as plain that no master or mistress can exercise authority effectively without the co-operation of their servants. And it is on the basis of the latter argument that much of the interest of the action turns on the various freedoms that servants enjoy within the contexts of domination to which they are subject. Accordingly, whereas there is a certain predictability about the behaviour of Emily [Brontë's] masters and mistresses, there is a complexity about her servants that makes their conduct especially worthy of discussion. Indeed, it is by virtue of that very complexity that the author puts the question of masters and servants, as it were, on the operating table, dealing with it not merely as a matter of economics but as a means of adding to our understanding of human nature. In other words, she invites us to consider, and perhaps even to question, a time-honoured system whose workings she astutely takes apart and lays bare for us. . . .

Servants Shape the Destiny of Their Masters

[Servants] influence events in the novel, and even shape its plot. To take two early instances: it is partly owing to Joseph's dilatoriness in fetching wine from the cellar that Lockwood gets into a fight with the dogs in Chapter 1, just as it is partly owing to Joseph's setting the dogs on Lockwood at the end of Chapter 2 that Lockwood spends the night in the oak-panelled room. Again, there is little doubt that Lockwood's second visit to the Heights is prompted principally by his finding a maid putting out his study fire at the Grange. But even a remark made casually by a servant can have important consequences for the plot. Thus Cathy's first encounter with Hareton is primarily due to the fact that 'one of the [Grange] maids mentioning the Fairy Cave, quite turned her head with a desire to fulfil this project: [. . .]'. Servants are also behind a good many of the reports and rumours that make up parts of Nelly Dean's narrative. Thus Nelly hears of Hareton's birth and the concomitant behaviour of his parents from the girl who brings breakfasts to her and others working in a hayfield; of Hindley's troubled relations with Heathcliff, shortly after the latter's return to Gimmerton, from Joseph; of Linton Heathcliff's conduct at the Heights from his father's (unnamed) housekeeper; of Cathy's way of life there under Heathcliff's guardianship from Zillah, prefacing her account, significantly enough, by saying, 'otherwise I should hardly know who was dead, and who living'. . . .

The Servants Are Insubordinate

The propensity of servants to talk to outsiders about the goings-on in their own households may be seen as an expression of the insubordination they are liable to show towards their superiors. There are, for example, occasions when Joseph is surly or defiant, slack or sardonic, in his attitude and demeanour towards those who are not his employers—Lockwood, Catherine, Edgar, Isabella, Cathy and Linton Heathcliff. He is sometimes even outspoken to his own master, as we note when, together with the curate, he 'reprimanded [Hindley's] carelessness when [Catherine and Heathcliff] absented themselves [from church on Sundays].' Nelly Dean herself, as well as now and then ignoring their requests or showing a lack of concern for them, can be downright disrespectful towards her superiors. Thus, aside from directing outbursts of anger against those belonging to other households, such as Heathcliff and his son Linton for trapping her and Cathy at the Heights, Nelly scolds her master Hindley for his mistreatment of Hareton and is, we are told later, 'many a time' spoken to 'sternly' by Edgar at the Grange for her 'pertness' to Catherine. But Edgar, too, no less than Catherine, is subject not only to Nelly's defiance, but also to her disobedience, notable instances of which later occur during the time she is looking after Cathy. Though some acts of disobedience on the part of servants may be adjudged reasonable, as when Nelly ignores Hindley's instruction to keep Catherine and Heathcliff locked out for the night, it is nevertheless interesting to note how ready the servants are to disobey their superiors when opportunity permits. . . . Lockwood's own subjection to the vagaries of domestics in both households and, more particularly, to the domination of his housekeeper Nelly Dean (as comically exemplified by her dictating the hours when he may dine) is doubtless intended as a symbolic caricature of the conflicts that so often arise in the novel between masters and servants.

The Servants' Understanding of the Master Complex and the Master's Weakness

Such conflicts seem due, at least in Nelly's case, partly to her finding herself obliged to be subservient to those to whom she was either an equal or over whom she had some power at one time, and partly to an awareness shared by other servants, namely, that the masters or mistresses served evince serious limitations of one kind or another. Thus we think of Hindley as a tyrannical, incompetent master; of Heathcliff as someone who, apart from being 'a cruel hard landlord to his tenants; [. . .],' is greatly feared as a master by all his servants, including the usually fearless Joseph; and of Catherine as a 'difficult' mistress, whose domination of people at the Grange extends even to allowing Isabella to 'be nothing in the house.' Moreover, in their strong desire to domineer over other people, each of these three characters seems beset by what might be termed a 'master complex'. In her diary, Catherine tells of

Hindley's bid to intimidate her and Heathcliff by saying, 'You forget you have a master here,' and, on account of the fateful Sunday evening visit to the Grange, his swearing that he 'will reduce [Heathcliff] to his right place.' Heathcliff's 'master complex' has more psychotic dimensions than Hindley's, as we realize when he gloatingly envisages his son's eventual power over the Linton family: 'I want the triumph of seeing *my* descendant fairly lord of their estates; my child hiring their children, to till their father's lands for wages—.' Catherine's 'master complex' is already manifest in childhood, inasmuch as she 'liked, exceedingly, to act the little mistress; using her hands freely, and commanding her companions.' It is also a perceptibly class-conscious one, as we see when, reprimanding Nelly for doing housework in the presence of herself and Edgar, she says: 'When company are in the house, servants don't commence scouring and cleaning in the room where they are!' That Catherine's 'master complex' is especially conspicuous after she has returned from her second convalescence at the Grange is evident both from her refusing to speak to Nelly 'save in the relation of a mere servant' and from her also putting Joseph 'under a ban' for lecturing her 'as if she were a little girl' because, as Nelly adds, she 'esteemed herself a woman, and our mistress [. . .].' Noteworthy too, in this respect, is Catherine's angry response to Nelly's having loudly voiced her objections to Heathcliff's amorous advances to Isabella: 'To hear you, people might think *you* were the mistress! [. . .] You want setting down in your right place!' At the other end of the spectrum, however, are Mr Earnshaw and Edgar Linton, who, though spoken of respectfully and affectionately by Nelly, come across as too weak with, or too trusting of, their subordinates, to be deemed exemplary masters. . . .

Nelly Has Significant Character Flaws

[For] all her skills as an observant and percipient [perceptive] narrator, Nelly betrays her limited intelligence not only through her propensity to be slow-witted, uncomprehending,

Portrait of a nineteenth-century household staff. Wuthering Heights *offers a detailed picture of the complex relationship between domestic servants and their masters.* © Time & Life Pictures/Getty Images.

forgetful and self-contradictory, but [also] through the presumptuousness and fallaciousness [untruth] of some of her ideas and arguments. Much more important, however, are the various references that Nelly makes throughout her narrative to her lies, prevarications, false promises, secretiveness, evasiveness and other forms of dishonesty, all of which amply underline her lack of moral integrity. This is not to suggest that Nelly has no sense of the difference between right and wrong but, rather, that she regards right and wrong as relative, and not absolute, concepts; that is to say, concepts which she considers right or wrong according to the particular circumstances she finds herself in. This may in turn account for her somewhat fuzzy notions about truth. For example, when, on arriving at the Heights in response to Isabella's letter, she assures Heathcliff that she has brought nothing for his wife, we note that, despite supplementing that detail with the words 'thinking it best to speak the truth at once,' she goes on to give Isabella an utterly garbled, if well-intended, version of Edgar's actual message to her. It may also account for the hypocrisy with which Nelly will give Edgar the impression of being 'a faithful servant' even while continuing to betray him. That is why it is especially during the tryst between the two principal lovers that the reader does well to recall that, in reaction to Heathcliff's earlier insistence that she arrange such a meeting for him, Nelly 'protested against playing that treacherous part in [her] employer's house.' It is, therefore, little wonder that Nelly seems scarcely able to understand the staunch loyalty which, for instance, Hareton consistently shows to Heathcliff, even beyond the latter's death.

At this juncture it might be asked whether Nelly's moral and mental shortcomings do not in some way derive from her role and function as a servant. It is interesting to note that, although she has more or less drifted into service, she seems never to have wished to be anything but a servant, and then only at the Heights or at the Grange. That Nelly might be said (like Joseph) to have a sort of vocation as a domestic is evident not only from her recurrent and respectful use of phrases entailing 'master' or 'mistress' and related terms such as 'my young lady', but from her apparent preference to live vicariously through her employers rather than to lead a life of her own, let alone cherish ambitions of any kind. This is partly implicit in the passivity informing her attitudes to her employers. For example, having told Lockwood that all the servants at the Heights except herself and Joseph gave notice on account of Hindley's 'tyrannical and evil conduct', she somewhat blandly rationalizes her decision to stay on by declaring that, having been his 'foster sister', she 'excused his behaviour more readily than a stranger would.' Again, in spite of refusing at first to accompany Catherine to the Grange on her marriage to Edgar, but then finding herself compelled to do so by Hindley, she rationalizes her acceptance as follows: 'And so, I had but one choice left, to do as I was ordered—.' Such passivity, unmistakable as it is for being expressed here in the guise of a fallacy, may, however, be thought hardly to square with the bold initiatives that Nelly takes in disregard of her employers' expectations. At the same time, Nelly seems to be well aware that the freedoms she permits herself are none the less exercised within, even determined by, the safe and secure confines of her particular employment. This may explain why, in anxious moments with her superiors, Nelly is quick to fall back on her role as servant, and even to take shelter in it. For example, when to her utter dismay she hears Cathy telling her father about her cousin Linton at the Heights, she recalls that, though 'not altogether sorry', she thought 'the burden of directing and warning would be more efficiently borne by [Edgar] than [herself].' Similarly, we note how, having failed with her threatening language to make the newly-wed Linton direct her to Cathy's room in the Heights, she tries to win him round by self-pityingly referring to herself as 'an elderly woman, and a servant merely.'

It may, then, be deduced from the words just quoted that one reason why Nelly gives scope to her character defects is that she (perhaps unconsciously) considers her social status too abject to bother herself unduly with questions of morality. Such an apparent lack of concern on her part seems confirmed by the fact that even her presentation as a Christian who relies heavily on the Bible for advice to pass on to her superiors does little, if anything, to deter her from her malpractices. In this connection, it is well to recollect here that two servants notable for their religiosity and their chapel-going, namely, Joseph and Zillah, come across as figures for whom morality is at best scarcely distinguishable from respectability. Certainly it would appear that Joseph has come to regard his efficiency, reliability and loyalty as a servant over many years as an excuse for him to overlook the basic principles of morality through his inveterate cantankerousness, maliciousness and misanthropy. Yet even for the other servants portrayed in the novel morality seems to have little relevance to their day-to-day existence. . . .

A Hierarchical Social System Breeds Bad Behavior

How far innate character or the hierarchical system is to blame for the unethical demeanour and attitude of the servants discussed above is a question that perhaps can only be answered tentatively. It is tempting, if not altogether justifiable, to conclude from evidence shown hitherto that being a servant brings out the worst in a human being, and that domestic service is likely to appeal most of all to the morally deficient. No doubt, the relationship between servant and employer is, by its very nature, seldom entirely disinterested or honourable. This idea is ironically confirmed by the presentation of a very minor figure in the novel, the groom Michael, through his willingness to betray his master Edgar Linton in order to be rewarded by Cathy with 'books and pictures' for enabling her to make her illicit journeys to the Heights. Yet at the same time as servants are liable to be disloyal to their employers, they cannot but play an important part in the maintenance of a household that is governed by a tyrannical head. Zillah, as we have already seen, is a striking case in point in that her outward obedience of Heathcliff, motivated as it is solely by fear, helps to preserve a fundamentally undesirable system of domination. Furthermore, we see how by working in a well-ordered household some servants may come to emulate the outlook of their masters and—as we may, for example, surmise from the vicious language with which Mr Linton's servant Robert addresses young Heathcliff in Chapter 6—thereby learn to exert over others the dominance to which they themselves have become habituated.

Another drawback of servants is that they tend to foster laziness and selfishness in their masters and mistresses, and, as we see in Isabella's case, to make them almost helpless. It is, accordingly, not without significance that Lockwood's somewhat unsympathetic presentation derives in some measure from his having apparently long taken it for granted that servants are not only a necessary part of everyday life but an indispensable luxury. This is ironically borne out when, for example, instead of finding out for himself on his return to the North how to get to Gimmerton, he simply 'directed [his] servant to inquire the way to the village.' Such a trifling use of a servant is perhaps enough of itself to indicate that, rather like Hindley and Heathcliff, Lockwood suffers from a 'master complex', and one which, towards the end of his narrative, may have been compounded both by memories of the insubordination he has had to endure from servants at the Heights and the Grange, and by his consciousness that he is after all only a tenant. Perhaps for that reason there is nothing quite so comical (among several other comical instances suggestive of his complex) as the occasion when, having quite unexpectedly turned up at the Grange in September 1802, he answers the old woman, who has just introduced herself as the person keeping the house, with this pompous reply: 'Well, I'm Mr Lockwood, the master.' . . .

Hope for the Master-Servant Relationship

It is . . . surely no coincidence that Cathy's relationship with Hareton should end happily at a time when, despite the latter's change of status from farmhand to 'the lawful master' of Wuthering Heights, as skilfully foreshadowed in Chapter 1 when Lockwood notices 'Hareton Earnshaw' carved above 'the principal door', of the building, the old hierarchical system as practised hitherto at the Heights and the Grange seems to be in marked abeyance. This is ironically underlined, first, when asked by Lockwood on his return to the Grange whether she is the housekeeper, the 'dame' (who, significantly enough, is smoking a pipe) replies: 'Eea, Aw keep th' hahse,' as if puzzled by his particular designation of her; and, soon afterwards, when, on ordering her to get the place ready for him, Lockwood observes her reactions as follows: 'She seemed willing to do her best; though she thrust the hearth-brush into the grates in mistake for the poker, and mal-appropriated several other articles of her craft; [. . .]'. As a sort of ironic dig at the scrupulously house-proud Nelly Dean, that detail seems symbolically to mark the dawn of an era in which, thanks to a youthful master who has known, perhaps better than any of his predecessors, what it is to be a servant in all but name, the relationship between masters and servants promises to become more wholesome than it is generally shown to have been so far in the narrative. Still, there are moments when relations between Nelly Dean and some of the main characters seem to evoke the charm that biographers have conveyed to us as to the friendship that Emily and her family enjoyed at Haworth Parsonage with their housekeeper Tabitha Aykroyd. Perhaps it is with this knowledge in mind that some readers might be readily disposed to look upon Nelly's triumphant survival as a servant at the end with no little sympathy and admiration.

Social Issues
in Literature

CHAPTER 3

Contemporary
Perspectives on
Class Conflict

The Major Social Conflict Is Now Between Classes, Not Races

Joel Kotkin

Joel Kotkin is the executive editor of the website NewGeography .com, a presidential fellow at Chapman University, and the author of The City: A Global History *and* The Next Hundred Million: America in 2050.

In this viewpoint, Kotkin argues that the trajectory of upward mobility in the United States has stalled. From the 1940s to the 1970s, those in the middle classes enjoyed the same percentage growth in income as the upper classes did. Since 1979 growth in prosperity has been restricted to the upper class, Kotkin claims, with the top 20 percent of taxpayers realizing almost 75 percent of all income gains over the next twenty-year period. As a result the gap between classes is growing, and class, not race, marks the new dividing line in American politics.

Barack Obama's ascension to the presidency [in 2009] won't end racism, but it does mean race is no longer the dominant issue in American politics. Instead, over the coming decades, class will likely constitute the major dividing line in our society—and the greatest threat to America's historic aspirations. This is a fundamental shift from the last century. Writing in the early 1900s, [African American sociologist and author] W.E.B. DuBois observed, "The problem of the 20th century is the problem of the color line." Developments in the ensuing years bore out this assertion. Indeed, before the 1960s, the decade of Barack Obama's birth, even the most talented people of color faced often insurmountable barriers to reaching their full potential. Today in a multiracial America, the path to success has opened up to an extent unimaginable in DuBois's time.

The Rise of the Black Middle Class

Obama's ascent reflects in particular the rise of the black bourgeoisie from tokens to a force at the heart of the meritocracy [a system in which success rests on personal achievement]. Since the late 1960s, the proportion of African-American households living in poverty has shrunk from 70 percent to 46 percent, while the black middle class has grown from 27 percent to 37 percent. Perhaps more remarkable, the percentage who are considered prosperous—earning more than $107,000 a year in 2007 dollars—expanded from 3 percent to 17 percent.

Yet as racial equity has improved, class disparities between rich and poor, between the ultra-affluent and the middle class, have widened. This gap transcends race. African-Americans and Latinos may tend, on average, to be poorer than whites or Asians, but stagnant or even diminishing incomes affect all ethnic groups. (Most housecleaners are white, for instance—and the same goes for other low-wage professions.) Divisions may not be as visible as during the Gilded Age [the late nineteenth century].

As [neoconservative American journalist] Irving Kristol once noted, "Who doesn't wear blue jeans these days?" You can walk into a film studio or software firm and have trouble distinguishing upper management from midlevel employees.

Upward Mobility Has Stalled

But from the 1940s to the 1970s, the American middle class enjoyed steadily increasing incomes that stayed on a par with those in the upper classes. Since then, wages for most workers have lagged behind. As a result, the relatively small number of Americans with incomes seven times or more above the poverty level have achieved almost all the recent gains in wealth.

Barack Obama is sworn in as president of the United States, January 20, 2009. Joel Kotkin argues that with the election of an African American president, the predominant issue in American politics is no longer race, but class. © Chuck Kennedy/Pool/Corbis.

Most disturbingly, the rate of upward mobility has stagnated overall, which means it is no easier for the poor to move up today than it was in the 1970s.

This disparity is strikingly evident in income data compiled by [international financial company] Citigroup, which shows that the top 1 percent of U.S. households now account for as much of the nation's total wealth—7 percent—as they did in 1913, when monopolistic business practices were the order of the day. Their net worth is now greater than that of the bottom 90 percent of the nation's households combined. The top 20 percent of taxpayers realized nearly three quarters of all income gains from 1979 to 2000.

Even getting a college degree no longer guarantees upward mobility. The implicit American contract has always been that with education and hard work, anyone can get ahead. But since 2000, young people with college educations—except those who go to elite colleges and graduate schools—have seen their wages decline. The deepening recession will make this worse. According to a 2008 survey by the National Association of Colleges and Employers, half of all companies plan to cut the number of new graduates they hire this year [2009], compared with last. But the problem goes well beyond the current crisis. For one thing, the growing number of graduates has flooded the job market at a time when many financially pressed boomers are postponing retirement. And college-educated workers today face unprecedented competition from skilled labor in other countries, particularly in the developing world.

The greatest challenge for Obama will be to change this trajectory for Americans under 30, who supported him by two to one. The promise that "anyone" can reach the highest levels of society is the basis of both our historic optimism and the stability of our political system. Yet even before the recession, growing inequality was undermining Americans' optimism about the future. In a 2006 [US market research and polling firm] Zogby poll, for example, nearly two thirds of adults did not think life would be better for their children. However inspirational the story of his ascent, Barack Obama will be judged largely by whether he can rebuild a ladder of upward mobility for the rest of America, too.

America Remains Divided by Class

Patrick Martin

Patrick Martin writes for the World Socialist Web Site, *a forum for socialist ideas published by the International Committee of the Fourth International.*

Martin contends in this selection that those who celebrate Sonia Sotomayor's ascension to the US Supreme Court as a victory for women and Hispanics are overlooking her true allegiance, which is to the financial upper class she has supported throughout her career. Sotomayor is just one in a long list of politicians who use a populist veneer of gender or ethnic identity to disguise their allegiance to the capitalist hierarchy. Martin defines the real political divide in America as that between capitalist owners and the workers they exploit.

The introduction of Sonia Sotomayor as President [Barack] Obama's first selection for the U.S. Supreme Court took place [in 2009] at a White House media event of a completely choreographed and stereotyped character. Such ceremonies have become an essential part of how America is governed. The less the political system is capable of actually responding to the needs and aspirations of working people, the more it must put on the pretense of concern, using biography as a substitute for policy.

Sotomayor Represents the Financial Upper Class

As always on such occasions, the nomination's "roll-out" was an unrestrained exercise in public tear-jerking. Led by President Obama, who based his own campaign on the marketing of a compelling personal "narrative," Sotomayor's elevation was presented as a triumph over all manner of adversity. There were tributes to the humble origins of the future Supreme Court justice, noting her hard-working immigrant parents, her poverty-stricken childhood in a South Bronx housing project, the death of her father when she was nine years old, and even her struggle with juvenile diabetes.

No doubt, it has not been an easy personal journey for Judge Sotomayor, and there can be little doubt that she is as tough as nails. However, amidst all the tributes to Judge Sotomayor's triumph, one cannot help but think about the conditions that confront the hundreds of thousands of South Bronx residents whom she left behind.

There is another element of Sotomayor's nomination that deserves analysis. Media coverage of the nomination, and the bulk of the political commentary, liberal and conservative, approving and hostile, focused on the fact that she would become the first Hispanic and third woman to take a seat on the highest U.S. court. The premise of both supporters and detractors was that Sotomayor's gender and ethnic origins were of decisive importance in evaluating her nomination and determining her likely course on the court.

Totally obliterated in this flood of commentary is the most fundamental social category in American society: class. Sotomayor will go to the Supreme Court, not as the representative or advocate of Hispanics, women or the socially disadvantaged more generally, but as the representative of a definite social class at the top of American society—the financial aristocracy whose interests she and every other federal judge, and the entire capitalist state machine, loyally serve and defend.

Only one "mainstream" bourgeois [middle-class capitalist] publication focused on this critical question. That was the *Wall Street Journal*, whose editorial page serves as a major voice of the ultra-right—denouncing the Sotomayor nomination in strident tones—but whose news pages explored her record as a well-paid commercial litigator and federal judge, on issues of direct interest to big business, including contract law, employment and property rights.

The newspaper quoted several Wall Street lawyers describing Sotomayor as a safe choice for corporate America. "There is no reason for the business community to be concerned," said one attorney. Barry Ostrager, a partner at [law firm] Simpson Thacher LLP who defended a unit of [global financial services company] J.P. Morgan Chase in a lawsuit over fraudulent pricing of initial public offerings [of stock], cited Sotomayor's role in an appeals court ruling barring the class-action suit. "That ruling demonstrated that in securities litigation, she is in the judicial mainstream," he told the *Journal*.

Social Class Is the Real Dividing Line

The American ruling class has gone further than any other in the world to suppress any public discussion of class. From the late 1940s on, the anti-communist witch-hunting associated with Senator Joseph McCarthy spearheaded a drive to effectively outlaw any public discussion of socialism, Marxism or the class divisions in American society.

In response to the social eruptions of the 1960s—the civil rights struggles and urban riots, the mass movement against the Vietnam War, and major struggles by the labor movement—the American bourgeoisie began to utilize identity politics to divide and confuse the mass opposition to its policies and block the emergence of the working class as an independent social force.

Black nationalism, "Chicano" nationalism, women's liberation and gay liberation all emerged, to name only the most heavily promoted forms of identity politics. In each case, real social grievances of significant sections of the American population were divorced from their connection to the socio-economic foundation—the division of society between the relative handful of capitalist owners of the means of production, and the vast majority of the population who must sell their labor power to make a living.

The Democratic Party became the principal vehicle for peddling the politics of race and gender, recruiting a layer of black, female and Hispanic politicians who engage in populist demagogy [employing popular prejudices and false promises to gain power] that uses race and gender to counterfeit an orientation to the interests of the oppressed masses of American society. But Republican administrations have learned how to engage in such posturing as well.

For the past 12 years for instance, under two Democratic presidents and one Republican, the post of U.S. Secretary of State has been occupied by, in succession, a white woman, a black man, a black woman, and a white woman. This exercise in "diversity" has not the slightest progressive significance. It has not democratized American foreign policy or made it one iota more conciliatory to the interests of the oppressed, either internationally or within the United States. Madeleine Albright, Colin Powell, Condoleezza Rice and Hillary Clinton are all representatives, not of "blacks" or "women," but of the most rapacious imperialist ruling class on the planet.

Barack Obama is the culmination of this process. Celebrated as the first African-American president, he has overseen the greatest handover of resources to the billionaires and Wall Street speculators in history. In the restructuring of the auto industry, with ever-escalating demands for cuts in jobs, pay and benefits for auto workers, he has set the stage for the greatest assault on the working class since the [Republican Ronald] Reagan administration smashed the PATCO [Professional Air Traffic Controllers Organization] air traffic controllers strike in 1981 and gave the signal for a nationwide campaign of wage-cutting and union-busting. In this, Obama demonstrates that the class he serves, not the color of his skin or his social origins, is the decisive political factor.

The political development of the American working class requires, first and foremost, the direct and open discussion of the class realities of American society. No country in the world is as deeply and intractably divided along economic lines as the United States, where the top 1 percent of the population owns 40 percent of the wealth and monopolizes 20 percent of the income. Any analysis of the political issues facing working people that does not take these class divisions as the fundamental reality is an exercise in deception and political stultification.

In Cross-Class Relationships, the Real Issue Is Power

Tamar Lewin

Tamar Lewin is an education reporter for The New York Times.

In the following viewpoint, Lewin asserts that in relationships between people from different socioeconomic classes, the spouse with more money usually wields the power. Although the differences in couples from diverse ethnic, racial, and religious backgrounds are obvious and can create conflict, the more subtle obstacles in cross-class marriages are equally challenging. Couples from different classes frequently have different educational levels and differing views on how to spend money, rear children, and spend their leisure time.

When Dan Croteau met Cate Woolner six years ago, he was selling cars at the Keene, N.H., Mitsubishi lot and she was pretending to be a customer, test driving a black Montero while she and her 11-year-old son, Jonah, waited for their car to be serviced.

Subtle but Important Differences

The test drive lasted an hour and a half. Jonah got to see how the vehicle performed in off-road mud puddles. And Mr. Croteau and Ms. Woolner hit it off so well that she later sent him a note, suggesting that if he was not involved with someone, not a Republican and not an alien life form, maybe they could meet for coffee. Mr. Croteau dithered about the propriety of dating a customer, but when he finally responded, they talked on the phone from 10 PM to 5 AM.

They had a lot in common. Each had two failed marriages and two children. Both love dancing, motorcycles, Bob Dylan, bad puns, liberal politics and National Public Radio.

But when they began dating, they found differences, too. The religious difference—he is Roman Catholic, she is Jewish—posed no problem. The real gap between them, both say, is more subtle: Mr. Croteau comes from the working class, and Ms. Woolner from money.

Mr. Croteau, who will be 50 in June, grew up in Keene, an old mill town in southern New Hampshire. His father was a factory worker whose education ended at the eighth grade; his mother had some factory jobs, too. Mr. Croteau had a difficult childhood and quit school at 16. He then left home, joined the Navy and drifted through a long series of jobs without finding any real calling. He married his pregnant 19-year-old girlfriend and had two daughters, Lael and Maggie, by the time he was 24.

"I was raised in a family where my grandma lived next door, my uncles lived on the next road over, my dad's two brothers lived next to each other, and I pretty much played with my cousins," he said. "The whole concept of life was that you should try to get a good job in the factory. My mother tried to encourage me. She'd say, 'Dan's bright; ask him a question.' But if I'd said I wanted to go to college, it would have been like saying I wanted to grow gills and breathe underwater."

He always felt that the rich people in town, "the ones with their names on the buildings," as he put it, lived in another world.

Ms. Woolner, 54, comes from that other world. The daughter of a doctor and a dancer, she grew up in a comfortable home in Hartsdale, N.Y., with the summer camps, vacations and college education that wealthy Westchester County families can take for granted. She was always uncomfortable with her money; when she came into a modest inheritance at 21, she ignored the monthly bank statements for several years, until she learned to channel her unease into philanthropy benefiting social causes. She was in her mid-30's and married to a psychotherapist when Isaac and Jonah were born.

"My mother's father had a Rolls-Royce and a butler and a second home in Florida," Ms. Woolner said, "and from as far back as I can remember, I was always aware that I had more than other people, and I was uncomfortable about it because it didn't feel fair. When I was little, what I fixated on with my girlfriends was how I had more pajamas than they did. So when I'd go to birthday sleepovers, I'd always take them a pair of pajamas as a present."

Marriages that cross class boundaries may not present as obvious a set of challenges as those that cross the lines of race or nationality. But in a quiet way, people who marry across class lines are also moving outside their comfort zones, into the uncharted territory of partners with a different level of wealth and education, and often, a different set of assumptions about things like manners, food, child-rearing, gift-giving and how to spend vacations. In cross-class marriages, one partner will usually have more money, more options and, almost inevitably, more power in the relationship.

It is not possible to say how many cross-class marriages there are. But to the extent that education serves as a proxy for class, they seem to be declining. Even as more people marry across racial and religious lines, often to partners who match them closely in other respects, fewer are choosing partners with a different level of education. While most of those marriages used to involve men marrying women with less education, studies have found, lately that pattern has flipped, so that by 2000, the majority involved women, like Ms. Woolner, marrying men with less schooling—the combination most likely to end in divorce.

"It's definitely more complicated, given the cultural scripts we've all grown up with," said Ms. Woolner, who has a master's degree in counseling and radiates a thoughtful sincerity. "We've all been taught it's supposed to be the man who has the money and the status and the power."

Bias Exists on Both Sides

When he met Ms. Woolner, Mr. Croteau had recently stopped drinking and was looking to change his life. But when she told him, soon after they began dating, that she had money, it did not land as good news.

"I wished she had waited a little," Mr. Croteau said. "When she told me, my first thought was, uh oh, this is a complication. From that moment I had to begin questioning my motivations. You don't want to feel like a gold digger. You have to tell yourself, here's this person that I love, and here's this quality that comes with the package. Cate's very generous, and she thinks a lot about what's fair and works very hard to level things out, but she also has a lot of baggage around that quality. She has all kinds of choices I don't have. And she does the lion's share of the decision-making."

Before introducing Ms. Woolner to his family, Mr. Croteau warned them about her background. "I said, 'Mom, I want you to know Cate and her family are rich,'" he recalled. "And she said, 'Well, don't hold that against her; she's probably very nice anyway.' I thought that was amazing."

There were biases on the other side too. Just last summer, Mr. Croteau said, when they were at Ms. Woolner's mother's house on Martha's Vineyard, his mother-in-law confessed to him that she had initially been embarrassed that he was a car salesman and worried that her daughter was taking him on as a kind of do-good project.

Still, the relationship moved quickly. Mr. Croteau met Ms. Woolner in the fall of 1998 and moved into her comfortable home in Northfield the next spring, after meeting her condition that he sell his gun.

Even before Mr. Croteau moved in, Ms. Woolner gave him money to buy a new car and pay off some debts. "I wanted to give him the money," she said. "I hadn't sweated it. I told him that this was money that had just come to me for being born into one class, while he was born into another class." And when he lost his job not long after, Ms. Woolner began paying him a monthly stipend—he sometimes refers to it as an allowance—that continued, at a smaller level, until last November [2004], when she quit her longstanding job at a local anti-poverty agency. She also agreed to pay for a $10,000 computer course that helped prepare him for his current job as a software analyst at the Cheshire Medical Center in Keene. From the beginning, the balance of power in the relationship was a sufficiently touchy issue that at Ms. Woolner's urging, a few months before their wedding in August 2001, they joined a series of workshops on cross-class relationships.

"I had abject terror at the idea of the group," said Mr. Croteau, who is blunt and intellectually engaging. "It's certainly an upper-class luxury to pay to tell someone your troubles, and with all the problems in the world, it felt a little strange to sit around talking about your relationship. But it was useful. It was a relief to hear people talk about the same kinds of issues we were facing, about who had power in the relationship and how they used it. I think we would have made it anyway, but we would have had a rockier time without the group."

It is still accepted truth within the household that Ms. Woolner's status has given her the upper hand in the marriage. At dinner one night, when her son Isaac said baldly, "I always think of my mom as having the power in the relationship," Mr. Croteau did not flinch. He is fully aware that in this relationship he is the one whose life has been most changed.

Confusing Differences

The Woolner-Croteau household is just up the hill from the groomed fields of Northfield Mount Hermon [NMH] prep school—a constant local reminder to Mr. Croteau of just how differently his wife's sons and his daughters have been educated. Jonah is now a senior there. Isaac, who also attended the school, is now back at Lewis & Clark College in Oregon after taking a couple of semesters away to study in India and to attend massage school while working in a deli near home.

By contrast, Mr. Croteau's adult daughters—who have never lived with the couple—made their way through the Keene public schools.

"I sometimes think Jonah and Isaac need a dose of reality, that a couple years in public school would have shown them something different," Mr. Croteau said. "On the other hand I sometimes wish I'd been able to give Maggie and Lael what they had. My kids didn't have the same kind of privilege and the same kind of schools. They didn't have teachers concerned about their tender growing egos. It was catch-as-catch-can for them, and that still shows in their personalities."

Mr. Croteau had another experience of Northfield Mount Hermon as well. He briefly had a job as its communications manager, but could not adjust to its culture.

"There were all these Ivy Leaguers," he said. "I didn't understand their nuances, and I didn't make a single friend there. In working-class life, people tell you things directly, they're not subtle. At N.M.H., I didn't get how they did things. When a vendor didn't meet the deadline, I called and said, 'Where's the job?' When he said, 'We bumped you, we'll have it next week,' I said, 'What do you mean, next week? We have a deadline, you can't do business like that.' It got back to my supervisor, who came and said, 'We don't yell at vendors.' The idea seemed to be that there weren't deadlines in that world, just guidelines."

Mr. Croteau says he is far more comfortable at the hospital. "I deal mostly with nurses and other computer nerds and they come from the same kind of world I do, so we know how to talk to each other," he said.

But in dealing with Ms. Woolner's family, especially during the annual visits to Martha's Vineyard, Mr. Croteau said, he sometimes finds himself back in class bewilderment, feeling again that he does not get the nuances. "They're incredibly gracious to me, very well bred and very nice," he said, "so much so that it's hard to tell whether it's sincere, whether they really like you."

Mr. Croteau still seems impressed by his wife's family, and their being among "the ones with their names on the buildings." It is he who shows a visitor the framed print of the old Woolner Distillery in Peoria, Ill., and, describing the pictures on the wall, mentions that this in-law went to Yale, and that one knew Gerald Ford.

Family Divisions

Mr. Croteau and Ms Woolner are not the only ones aware of the class divide within the family; so are the two sets of children.

Money is continually tight for Lael Croteau, 27, who is in graduate school in educational administration at the University of Vermont, and Maggie, 25, who is working three jobs while in her second year of law school at American University. At restaurants, they ask to have the leftovers wrapped to take home.

Neither could imagine taking a semester off to try out massage school, as Isaac did. They are careful about their manners, their plans, their clothes.

"Who's got money, who doesn't, it's always going on in my head," Maggie said. "So I put on the armor. I have the bag. I have the shirt. I know people can't tell my background by looking."

The Croteau daughters are the only ones among 12 first cousins who made it to college. Most of the others married and had babies right after high school.

"They see us as different, and sometimes that can hurt," Maggie said.

The daughters walk a fine line. They are deeply attached to their mother, who did most of their rearing, but they are also attracted to the Woolner world and its possibilities. Through holidays and Vineyard vacations, they have come to feel close not only to their stepbrothers, but also to Ms. Woolner's sisters' children, whose pictures are on display in Lael's house in Vermont. And they see, up close, just how different their upbringing was.

"Jonah and Isaac don't have to worry about how they dress, or whether they'll have the money to finish college, or anything," Lael said. "That's a real luxury. And when one of the little kids asks, 'Why do people sneeze?' their mom will say, 'I don't know; that's a great question. Let's go to the museum, and check it out.' My mom is very smart and certainly engages us on many levels, but when we asked a difficult question, she'd say, 'Because I said so.'"

The daughters' lives have been changed not only by Ms. Woolner's warm, stable presence, but also by her gifts of money for snow tires or books, the family vacations she pays for and her connections. One of Ms. Woolner's cousins, a Washington lawyer, employs Maggie both at her office and as a housesitter.

For Ms. Woolner's sons, Mr. Croteau's arrival did not make nearly as much difference. They are mostly oblivious of the extended Croteau family, and have barely met the Croteau cousins, who are close to their age and live nearby but lead quite different lives. Indeed, in early February, while Ms. Woolner's Isaac was re-adjusting to college life, Mr. Croteau's nephew, another 20-year-old Isaac who had enlisted in the Marines right after high school, was shot in the face in Fallujah, Iraq, and shipped to Bethesda Medical Center in Maryland. Isaac and Jonah are easygoing young men, neither of whom has any clear idea what he wants to do in life. "For a while I've been trying to find my passion," Jonah said. "But I haven't been passionately trying to find my passion."

Isaac fantasizes about opening a brewery-cum-performance-space, traveling through South America or operating a sunset massage cruise in the Caribbean. He knows he is on such solid ground that he can afford fantasy.

"I have the most amazing safety net a person could have," he said, "incredible, loving, involved and wealthy parents."

The Difficulties and Confusion Will Always Be Present

On the rare occasions when they are all together, the daughters get on easily with the sons, though there are occasional tensions. Maggie would love to have a summer internship with a human rights group, but she needs paid work and when she graduates, with more than $100,000 of debt, she will need a law firm job, not one with a nonprofit. So when Isaac one day teased her as being a sellout, she reminded him that it was a lot easier to live your ideals when you did not need to make money to pay for them.

And there are moments when the inequalities within the family are painfully obvious.

"I do feel the awkwardness of helping Isaac buy a car, when I'm not helping them buy a car," Ms. Woolner said of the daughters. "We've talked about that. But I also have to be aware of overstepping. Their mother's house burned down, which was awful for them and for her and I really wanted to help. I took out my checkbook and I didn't know what was appropriate. In the end I wrote a $1,500 check. Emily Post doesn't deal with these situations."

She and Mr. Croteau remain conscious of the class differences between them, and the ways in which their lives have been shaped by different experiences.

On one visit to New York City, where Ms. Woolner's mother lives in the winter, Ms. Woolner lost her debit card and felt anxious about being disconnected, even briefly, from her money.

For Mr. Croteau, it was a strange moment. "She had real discomfort, even though we were around the corner from her mother, and she had enough money to do anything we were likely to do, assuming she wasn't planning to buy a car or a diamond all of a sudden," he said. "So I didn't understand the problem. I know how to walk around without a safety net. I've done it all my life."

Both he and his wife express pride that their marriage has withstood its particular problems and stresses.

"I think we're always both amazed that we're working it out," Ms. Woolner said.

But almost from the beginning they agreed on an approach to their relationship, a motto now engraved inside their wedding rings: "Press on regardless."

Class Distinctions Extend to Social Networks

Breeanna Hare

Breeanna Hare is a writer and producer at CNN.com.

In this selection, Hare discusses the significant class differences among the users of social networks: Myspace tends to attract those at the bottom of the class pyramid, Facebook has a more prosperous user base, and LinkedIn has the most affluent subscribers. Some researchers worry that the tendency of people to migrate to sites where members of their own class hang out serves only to entrench existing class boundaries, Hare reports.

Like a lot of people, Anna Owens began using MySpace more than four years ago to keep in touch with friends who weren't in college.

There Is an Online Class Divide

But soon she felt too old for the social-networking site, and the customizable pages with music that were fun at first began to annoy her. By the time she graduated from the University of Puget Sound, Owens' classmates weren't on MySpace—they were on Facebook.

Throughout graduate school and beyond, as her network began to expand, Owens ceased using MySpace altogether. Facebook had come to represent the whole of her social and professional universe.

"MySpace has one population, Facebook has another," said the 26-year-old, who works for an affordable-housing nonprofit in San Francisco, California. "Blue-collar, part-time workers might like the appeal of MySpace more—it definitely

Breeanna Hare, "Does Your Social Class Determine Your Online Social Network?," CNN.com, October 13, 2009. Reproduced by permission.

depends on who you meet and what they use; that's what motivates people to join and stay interested."

Is there a class divide online? Research suggests yes. A recent study by market research firm Nielsen Claritas found that people in more affluent demographics are 25 percent more likely to be found friending on Facebook, while the less affluent are 37 percent more likely to connect on MySpace.

More specifically, almost 23 percent of Facebook users earn more than $100,000 a year, compared to slightly more than 16 percent of MySpace users. On the other end of the spectrum, 37 percent of MySpace members earn less than $50,000 annually, compared with about 28 percent of Facebook users.

MySpace users tend to be "in middle-class, blue-collar neighborhoods," said Mike Mancini, vice president of data product management for Nielsen, which used an online panel of more than 200,000 social media users in the United States in August [2009]. "They're on their way up, or perhaps not college educated."

By contrast, Mancini said: "Facebook [use] goes off the charts in the upscale suburbs," driven by a demographic that for Nielsen is represented by white or Asian married couples between the ages of 45–64 with kids and high levels of education.

Even more affluent are users of Twitter, the microblogging site, and Linkedin, a networking site geared to white-collar professionals. Almost 38 percent of Linkedin users earn more than $100,000 a year.

Nielsen also found a strong overlap between those who use Facebook and those who use Linkedin, Mancini said.

Nielsen isn't the first to find this trend. Ethnographer danah boyd, who does not capitalize her name, said she watched the class divide emerge while conducting research of American teens' use of social networks in 2006.

A young woman checks her Facebook page. Studies show that social networking demographics are sharply divided by class and that socioeconomic boundaries often extend to life on the Internet. © Chris Rout/Alamy.

When she began, she noticed the high school students all used MySpace, but by the end of the school year, they were switching to Facebook.

When boyd asked why, the students replied with reasons similar to Owens: "the features were better; MySpace is dangerous and Facebook is safe; my friends are here," boyd recalled.

And then, boyd said, "a young woman, living in a small historical town in Massachusetts said to me, 'I don't mean to be a racist or anything, but MySpace is like, ghetto.'" For boyd, that's when it clicked.

"It's not a matter of choice between Facebook and MySpace, it was a movement to Facebook from MySpace," she said, a movement that largely included the educated and the upper-class.

So why do our online worlds, unencumbered by what separates us in daily life, reflect humans' tendency to stick with what—and who—they know?

Social Networking Divides Mirror Everyday Divides

A lot of it has to do with the disparate beginnings of MySpace and Facebook, said Adam Ostrow, editor-in-chief of *Mashable*, a blog about social media. Facebook originated at Harvard University and was limited at first to students at approved colleges before opening itself to the public in September 2006.

MySpace, on the other hand, had a "come one, come all" policy and made a mad dash towards monetization [turning the site into a moneymaker], Ostrow said. "They used a lot of banner ads without regard to the quality, and it really diminished the value [of the site] for the more tech-savvy demographic."

And while the Internet can build bridges between people on opposite sides of the globe, we still tend to connect with the same people through online social networks who we connect with offline, said technology writer and blogger Sarah Perez.

"It's effectively a mirror to our real world," she told CNN. "Social networks are the online version of what kids do after school."

These social-networking divides are worrisome to boyd, who wrote "Taken Out of Context: American Teen Sociality in Networked Publics." Instead of allowing us to cross the boundaries that exist in our everyday lives, these online class differences threaten to carry those boundaries into the future.

"The social-network infrastructure is going to be a part of everything going forward, just like [Web] search is," boyd said. "The Internet is not this great equalizer that rids us of the problems of the physical world—the internet mirrors and magnifies them. The divisions that we have in everyday life are going to manifest themselves online."

Jason Kaufman, a research science fellow with the Berkman Center for Internet and Society at Harvard University, examined the Facebook profiles of a group of college students over four years and found that even within Facebook, there's evidence of self-segregation.

Multiracial students tended to have more Facebook friends than students of other backgrounds and were often the sole connection between white and black circles, Kaufman said.

Nonetheless, Kaufman feels that social networks may one day help us overcome our instinct to associate with those who share our income level, education, or racial background.

"I think it's fair to say that the Web has great potential to at least mitigate everyday tendencies towards self-segregation and social exclusion," Kaufman said. "In some ways, [Facebook] levels the playing field of friendship stratification. In the real world, you have very close friends and then there are those you just say "Hi" to when you pass them on the street.

"The playing field is a lot more level in that you can find yourself having a wall-to-wall exchange with just an acquaintance. If you pick up the unlikely friend, not of your race or income bracket, the network may [help you] establish a more active friendship than if you met them in real life."

But MySpace's users still find something appealing about MySpace that they don't about Facebook, and it may have nothing to do with class or race, blogger Perez said.

"It's not just the demographics that have people picking one over the other," Perez said. "It also comes down to what activities you like. If you like music, you'll still be on MySpace. If you're more into applications, then you might go to Facebook because you're addicted to Mafia Wars or whatever."

Twitter Is the Most Open Network

In the end, boyd isn't as concerned about the reasons behind these divisions online as she is about the consequences of people only networking within their chosen social-media groups.

"Friendships and family relationships are socially divided; people self-segregate to deal with racism sometimes," she said. "Okay, fine: We've made a decision to self-segregate; but what happens when politicians go on Facebook and think they're reaching the whole public? What happens when colleges only go on Facebook to promote?"

When and if that does happen, *Mashable*'s Ostrow said, we'll know perhaps we've given social networks more credit than they're worth. "When it comes to information, I don't think social networks are the best source for that. The Internet is so open," said Ostrow, who believes users would go beyond their networks to search out information online.

If you're looking to branch out of your social network box, your best option may be Twitter. Nielsen's survey didn't find a dominant social class on Twitter as much as they found a geographical one: Those who use Twitter are more likely to live in an urban area where there's greater access to wireless network coverage, Mancini said.

"The simplicity of Twitter definitely creates less of a divide, because it's not a relationship like it is on MySpace or Facebook," Ostrow said. "If you live in the middle of nowhere or you live in a city, you can follow anyone about anything."

For Further Discussion

1. In Chapter 1 critic Tom Winnifrith comments that unlike most Victorian writers, Emily Brontë creates characters who are multidimensional and who defy stereotyping. Describe the contradictory characteristics of some of the major characters in *Wuthering Heights*.

2. In Chapter 2 Beth Newman maintains that to appreciate *Wuthering Heights*, it is important that students understand it in the context of the Industrial Revolution that swept through England in the first half of the nineteenth century. What changes did the Industrial Revolution bring to Victorian society? How are they reflected in *Wuthering Heights*?

3. In Chapter 2 both Terry Eagleton and Daniela Garofalo offer conflicting views on the character of Heathcliff. Eagleton sees Heathcliff as a rebel against capitalist society, while Garofalo sees in him the embodiment of the capitalistic impulse. Who do you agree with and why?

4. In Chapter 3 Breeanna Hare writes that most people use social networks to communicate with people who are similar to them. If you participate in a social network, is this your experience? Do your virtual friends differ in any ways from your real-life friends? If so, have you gained any insights from people who have different experiences?

For Further Reading

Jane Austen, *Emma: A Novel*. London: John Murray, 1815.

——, *Pride and Prejudice: A Novel*. London: Thomas Egerton, 1813.

——, *Sense and Sensibility: A Novel*. London: Thomas Egerton, 1811.

Anne Brontë, *Agnes Grey*. London: T.C. Newby, 1847.

——, *The Tenant of Wildfell Hall*. London: T.C. Newby, 1848.

Charlotte Brontë, *Jane Eyre: An Autobiography*. London: Smith, Elder & Co., 1847.

——, *The Professor: A Tale*. London: Smith, Elder & Co., 1857.

——, *Shirley: A Tale*. London: Smith, Elder & Co., 1849.

——, *Villette*. London: Smith, Elder & Co., 1853.

Charlotte Brontë, Emily Brontë, and Anne Brontë, *Poems by Currer, Ellis, and Acton Bell*. London: Aylott & Jones, 1846.

Emily Brontë, *The Complete Poems of Emily Jane Brontë*. Ed. C.W. Hatfield. New York: Columbia University Press, 1941.

Charles Dickens, *Great Expectations*. London: Chapman and Hall, 1861.

Daphne Du Maurier, *My Cousin Rachel*. London: Victor Gollancz, 1951.

——, *Rebecca*. London: Victor Gollancz, 1938.

Thomas Hardy, *Tess of the d'Urbervilles: A Pure Woman Faithfully Presented*. London: Osgood, McIlvaine, 1891.

Bibliography

Books

Miriam Allott, ed.   *The Brontës: The Critical Heritage.*
London: Routledge & Kegan Paul,
1974.

Kathleen R.   *America's New Working Class: Race,*
Arnold   *Gender, and Ethnicity in a Biopolitical*
Age. University Park: University of
Pennsylvania State Press, 2008.

Juliet Barker   *The Brontës.* London: Weidenfeld &
Nicholson, 1994.

Mark D. Brewer   *Split: Class and Cultural Divides in*
and Jeffrey M.   *American Politics.* Washington, DC:
Stonecash   CQ Press, 2006.

Emily Brontë   *Wuthering Heights: Complete,*
Authoritative Text with Biographical
and Historical Contexts, Critical
History, and Essays from Five
Contemporary Critical Perspectives.
Ed. Linda H. Peterson. Boston: St.
Martin's Press, Bedford Books, 1992.

Stevie Davies   *Emily Brontë.* Bloomington: Indiana
University Press, 1988.

Herbert Dingle   *The Mind of Emily Brontë.* London:
M. Brian and O'Keeffe, 1974.

Alastair G.   *"Wuthering Heights": An Anthology of*
Everitt, comp.   *Criticism.* London: Frank Cass & Co.,
1967.

Inga-Stina Ewbank	*Their Proper Sphere: A Study of the Brontë Sisters as Early Victorian Female Novelists.* Cambridge, MA: Harvard University Press, 1966.
Winifred Gérin	*Emily Brontë: A Biography.* Oxford: Clarendon Press, 1972.
Sandra Gilbert and Susan Gubar	*The Madwoman in the Attic: The Woman Writer and the Nineteenth-Century Imagination.* New Haven: Yale University Press, 1978.
James Kavanagh	*Emily Brontë.* Rereading Literature Series. London: Basil Blackwell, 1985.
Richard Lettis and William E. Morris	*A "Wuthering Heights" Handbook.* New York: Odyssey Press, 1961.
Sara Mills and Lynn Pearce	*Feminist Readings/Feminists Reading,* 2nd ed. New York: Prentice Hall/Harvester Wheatsheaf, 1996.
Jenny Oldfield	*"Jane Eyre" and "Wuthering Heights": A Study Guide.* London: Heinemann Educational Books, 1976.
Lyn Pykett	*Emily Brontë.* Women Writers Series. Basingstoke, England: Macmillan, 1989.
Charles Simpson	*Emily Brontë.* Folcroft, PA: Folcroft Library Editions, 1977.
Muriel Spark and Derek Stanford	*Emily Brontë: Her Life and Work.* London: P. Owen, 1953.

| Patsy Stoneman, ed. | *Wuthering Heights*. New Casebook Series. Basingstoke, England: Macmillan, 1993. |
| Tom Winnifrith | *The Brontës*. London: Macmillan, 1977. |

Periodicals

Nancy Armstrong	"Emily's Ghost: The Cultural Politics of Victorian Fiction, Folklore, and Photography," *Novel: A Forum on Fiction*, vol. 25, no. 3, Spring 1992.
Bruce Bartlett	"Class Struggle in America?" *Commentary*, vol. 120, no. 1, July–August 2005.
Irving M. Buchen	"Metaphysical and Social Evolution in *Wuthering Heights*," *Victorian Newsletter*, vol. 31, Spring 1967.
V. Buckley	"Passion and Control in *Wuthering Heights*," *Southern Review*, vol. 1, 1964.
C.W. Davis	"A Reading of *Wuthering Heights*," *Essays in Criticism*, vol. 19, 1969.
Emilio DeGrazia	"The Ethical Dimension of *Wuthering Heights*," *Midwest Quarterly*, vol. 19, Winter 1978.
James Hafley	"The Villain in *Wuthering Heights*," *Nineteenth-Century Fiction*, vol. 13, December 1958.

Myungjin Kim "An Apology for Nelly: From the Viewpoint of Her Social Relations and Class," *British and American Fiction to 1900*, vol. 15, no. 2, Fall 2008.

Margaret Lenta "Capitalism or Patriarchy and Immoral Love: A Study of *Wuthering Heights*," *Theoria: A Journal of Studies in the Arts, Humanities and Social Sciences*, vol. 62, May 1984.

Thomas Maser "What Is the Matter with Emily Jane?: Conflicting Impulses in *Wuthering Heights*," *Nineteenth-Century Fiction*, vol. 17, June 1962.

T.K. Meier "*Wuthering Heights* and Violations of Class," *Brontë Society Transactions*, vol. 15, 1968.

Carol Ohmann "Emily Brontë in the Hands of Male Critics," *College English*, vol. 32, May 1971.

Maja-Lisa Von Sneidern "*Wuthering Heights* and the Liverpool Slave Trade," *ELH*, vol. 62, no. 1, Spring 1995.

Patricia Yaeger "Violence in the Sitting Room: *Wuthering Heights* and the Woman's Novel," *Genre*, vol. 21, 1988.

Internet Sources

Stanley Fish   "'Law and Order' Probably Doesn't
                  Like You," *New York Times*, August 2,
                  2010. Opinionator.blogs.nytimes
                  .com.

Matthew Parris   "The 'Underclass' Is a Consequence
                  of Social Mobility's Success, Not of
                  Its Decline," *Spectator*, July 4, 2007.
                  www.spectator.co.uk.

Index